D1272727

THE LIFE OF
HARRIET
TUBMAN

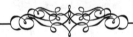

Moses of the
Underground
Railroad

Anne Schraff

 Enslow Publishers, Inc.
40 Industrial Road
Box 398
Berkeley Heights, NJ 07922
USA
http://www.enslow.com

Copyright © 2015 by Anne Schraff

All rights reserved.

Originally published as *Harriet Tubman: Moses of the Underground Railroad* in 2001.

No part of this book may be reproduced by any means
without the written permission of the publisher.

Library of Congress Cataloging-in-Publication Data

Schraff, Anne E.
    The life of Harriet Tubman : Moses of the Underground Railroad / Anne
    Schraff.
        pages cm. — (Legendary African Americans)
    Includes bibliographical references and index.
    ISBN 978-0-7660-6137-8
    1. Tubman, Harriet, 1820?–1913—Juvenile literature. 2. Slaves—United
    States—Biography—Juvenile literature. 3. African American women—
    Biography—Juvenile literature. 4. African Americans—Biography—Juvenile
    literature. 5. Underground Railroad—Juvenile literature. I. Title.
    E444.T82S362 2014
    306.3'62092—dc23
    [B]

                                    2013049810

Future editions:
Paperback ISBN: 978-0-7660-6138-5
EPUB ISBN: 978-0-7660-6139-2
Single-User PDF ISBN: 978-0-7660-6140-8
Multi-User PDF ISBN: 978-0-7660-6141-5

Printed in the United States of America
072014 HF Group, North Manchester, IN
10 9 8 7 6 5 4 3 2 1

To Our Readers:
We have done our best to make sure all Internet addresses in this book were active and
appropriate when we went to press. However, the author and the publisher have no control
over and assume no liability for the material available on those Internet sites or on other
Web sites they may link to. Any comments or suggestions can be sent by e-mail to
comments@enslow.com or to the address on the back cover.

Illustration Credits: Enslow Publishers, Inc., pp. 23, 49; Library of Congress,
p. 4.

Cover Illustration: Library of Congress

CONTENTS

For sixteen years, Harriet Tubman risked her freedom and her life to help almost three hundred slaves escape the shackles of forced labor.

Chapter 1

THE NEXT TIME MOSES COMES

Josiah Bailey was a handsome, muscular Maryland slave, valued as much for his intelligence as for his strength. He was a skilled farmer entrusted with helping to manage the plantation where he worked. A quiet man, Bailey probably would have spent his whole life in slavery except for an incident in November 1856. That incident made him seek out Harriet Tubman, a runaway slave known to thousands as Moses. Their meeting changed Bailey's life.

Bailey had been hired out by his master to another plantation owner, William Hughlett, for many years. It was common for masters to rent out their slaves to others when they were not needed on the home plantation. This brought extra income to the masters who owned the slaves.

Hughlett decided he wanted to buy Bailey and train him to be an overseer on his plantation. Hughlett paid $2,000 at a time when good field hands were selling for about $1,500. But on the fall morning when he arrived to take possession of Josiah Bailey, his newly purchased slave, Hughlett made a serious mistake.

Bailey was in his small cabin eating breakfast when Hughlett shouted for him to come out. Bailey left his meal and dutifully presented himself to his new master.

"Now Joe," Hughlett demanded, "strip, and take a licking."[1]

During the times Hughlett had rented Bailey, the slave had always done excellent work. Hughlett had never found reason to criticize Bailey. What had Bailey done to deserve this? When he asked Hughlett why he was getting a beating, the white man replied, "You always worked well, but you belong to me now. I always begin by giving them [new slaves] a good licking. . . . Now strip and take it."[2]

Bailey obeyed. He stripped and took a terrible beating. But the injustice and humiliation of the flogging made Bailey decide that this would be his final beating. As soon as he could, he sought out Harriet Tubman's father. "Next time Moses comes," Bailey told him, "let me know."[3]

"Moses" was Harriet Tubman, a small, ordinary-looking Maryland woman, a runaway slave herself. She secretly met with escaping slaves and led them northward to freedom along a route she knew by heart. She was familiar with every mile of land between Maryland and Canada.[4] She used one of the many trails leading northward toward freedom. These routes were known as the Underground Railroad, and Tubman was one of its most effective and fearless conductors.

Bailey continued to work for Hughlett until one night when word spread through the plantation that Tubman was in the area to shepherd another group of fugitive slaves to freedom. Josiah Bailey joined the group of runaways.

Because Bailey was so valuable, rewards of $1,000 and then $2,000 were offered for his capture and return. But Tubman was extremely clever.[5] She led Bailey and the others as she always led the runaways, in groups of four or five. They rested by day and traveled by night, passing out of Cambridge, Maryland, over the Choptank River bridge, through the Delaware towns of Camden, Dover, Smyrna, and Odessa. Tubman and her charges always found a warm welcome at the home of Thomas Garrett in Wilmington.[6] Garrett was a friend of Tubman's who actively opposed slavery.

After resting at Garrett's home, Tubman led Bailey and the others to a wagon carrying some bricklayers. She had hired them as a decoy for her runaway slaves. Tubman always planned well ahead, using a wide variety of imaginative covers to disguise her caravans of slaves. The bricklayers made room for the slaves among them, and then the bricklayers began singing and shouting merrily as the wagon rolled over a bridge where the local sheriffs frequently searched passing wagons for slaves. The runaways huddled in the bottom of the wagon by the feet of the raucous bricklayers, and the wagon was waved through without a close inspection. Once again, one of Tubman's ruses had worked.

Tubman then led her little group through Chester, Pennsylvania, into Philadelphia, then to upstate New York. But Bailey began to worry that in spite of Tubman's skill they would all be caught and returned to slavery. He could not quite believe Moses could pull this off. Later, Tubman recalled Bailey's depression this way: "Joe was silent; he talked no more; he sang no more."[7]

They were almost to Canada and freedom, but there was one final hurdle. Tubman led them onto a train that would cross a bridge into Canada. As they crossed over into Canada, Tubman ran to Josiah Bailey, grabbed his shoulder and cried, "You shook the lion's paw, Joe. You're free!"[8] Tubman called entering Canada, where slavery had been abolished, "shaking the lion's paw."

Now, at last, Josiah Bailey was a free man. Everyone gathered around him. Tubman could not see Joe during the wild celebration, but she could hear his joyous singing. After that, Tubman saw Bailey several times when he was living in Canada—happy, industrious, and free.[9]

Josiah Bailey was just one of about three hundred slaves Harriet Tubman would lead to freedom.[10]

Chapter 2

LIKE A WEED

When Harriet Tubman was a grown-up, she looked back on her childhood and recalled, "I grew up like a neglected weed, ignorant of liberty, having no experience of it."[1]

Harriet's mother, Harriet Greene, was nicknamed Rit. When Rit was ten years old, she and her mother arrived at the Edward Brodas plantation. Later Rit married Benjamin Ross, a skilled lumberman. Ross supervised a crew of slaves cutting oak, cypress, and poplar trees and then hauling them to the shipyards of Baltimore. Ross was said to have strange powers. Harriet Tubman later said that her father could "predict the weather" and that he "foretold the Mexican War."[2] Harriet's parents were respected as clever, honest, and religious people with a strong sense of family loyalty.[3]

Harriet was born around 1820—nobody knows for sure because her birth was not recorded. Her parents could neither read nor write. They did not even know what month it was. They told time by the seasons: summer, winter, planting time, and harvest time. When slave children were born, friends and relatives came to visit the mother, and their memories served as birth notices.

Harriet and Benjamin Ross named their daughter Araminta, and as a small child she was called Minty. Sometime during her later childhood she decided to use her mother's name—Harriet.[4] Little Harriet was the middle child of eleven children born to the Rosses. There are no dependable records revealing all their names or how many survived to adulthood.

Harriet was born in the tiny community of Bucktown, in Dorchester County, Maryland, about sixty miles south of Baltimore. The so-called Mason-Dixon line that separated the slave-owning state of Maryland from free Pennsylvania was one hundred miles to the north.

The Rosses lived in one of the slave cabins set back from the Brodas house. The cabins had one room and no windows. Chinks in the logs of the cabins were packed with mud to keep out the cold and the rain. A clay-daubed chimney kept the cabin warmed in winter, but there was always a smoky smell in the room.

Harriet and her family lived on slaves' rations of food, such as cornmeal, smoked herring, and pork. The slave cabin did not have an oven, so cornmeal was mixed with flour and placed between two leaves to cook outside in an open fire. The result was called ashcake. Little children usually ate cornmeal mush.

For young Harriet, as for all slave children, childhood lasted only about five years. During her early years she slept on a straw pallet and ran barefoot after rabbits in the woods. Children played together under the supervision of an elderly slave woman. But when Harriet was about six, her childhood ended.

The fortunes of the Brodas family had been in decline since about 1824, when Edward Brodas took over the plantation from his parents. Most of the tobacco plantations in Maryland had worn out the soil by planting the same crop year after year. Now they needed other sources of income. Brodas grew apples, wheat, rye, and corn. He cut and sold timber from the woodland on his 442 acres.

With nine children to support, the Brodas family was eager to raise cash. One way to make quick money was to sell off or hire out the slaves. Even a slave as young as Harriet could be a source of income. Prospective employers began to arrive at the Brodas plantation to look over the slaves, including Harriet.

One day a white couple came to the Brodas plantation in search of a cheap young slave to help the wife with her weaving business. The husband, James Cook, chose Harriet, so off went the little girl in the white couple's wagon. Harriet had never been away from home before. Now she was being separated from all she knew and loved, going into an uncertain future.

At the Cook house, Harriet slept on the kitchen floor, and she often ate the table scraps with the family dogs. Harriet was put to work helping to wind yarn, but the work made her sneeze and cough so much she could not continue. Harriet was then given a new task—helping Mr. Cook watch his muskrat traps. Harriet spent long days wading in the icy river, checking the traplines for animals. Soon she came down with a severe cough and high fever. Harriet had to be sent home to the Brodas plantation, where her mother nursed her back to health.

Edward Brodas was eager to rent Harriet out again as soon as she was well. Harriet's two older sisters, Linah and Sophia, had already been sold to work on huge cotton and rice plantations in what was called the New South—Mississippi, Louisiana, and Alabama. Slave conditions were much harsher there than in Maryland. Harriet was too young to be sold, so Brodas rented her out again, this time to a couple with a small baby. They needed a nursemaid and a housekeeper and they did not want to pay very much. Once again Harriet went off with a white couple to a strange house.

Harriet was about seven by then, a sturdy little girl who did her best to keep the baby content and the rooms dusted. Still, she did not satisfy her new mistress. Harriet could not keep the house clean enough, and she was whipped for her failure. Harriet was often whipped by people who rented her. Her neck grew crisscrossed with scars that remained with her for the rest of her life.[5]

Tubman later said she had "heard" that there were good masters and mistresses, but she had not come across any.[6]

Harriet learned to dress in as many pieces of clothing as she could find—the thicker the better—to protect her skin from the lash.[7] Knowing that her angry mistress wanted to make sure she was inflicting pain, Harriet howled loudly, even when the padding protected her.[8] Later on, when Harriet was invited to join the family in prayer, she always stood by herself on the landing of the stairs. "I prayed to God," she remembered, "to make me strong and able to fight and that's what I've always prayed for ever since."[9]

Harriet was a curious, adventurous child. She had never tasted sweets, so when she saw a lump of sugar one day on her mistress's table, she could not resist the temptation to snatch it up. The woman saw the theft and chased Harriet as she fled outside. Harriet ran her fastest, finally taking refuge in a place she thought would not be searched—the pigpen. She hid there for days with nothing to eat but the potato peelings she grabbed from the pigs. Finally she had to come out, and that day she got the whipping she had dreaded. Then, once again, she was sent back to the Brodas plantation as an unsatisfactory slave.

None of Harriet's housekeeping and child care jobs had worked out well. She just did not take to those kinds of tasks. Harriet did much better at outdoor work, and she was becoming a very strong girl.

In the summer of 1835, when Harriet was about fifteen, she was shucking corn for her master when an incident occurred that would change her life. A runaway slave, fleeing his master, ran right past Harriet as she worked. The overseer was hot on the boy's trail. When the overseer saw

Harriet, he shouted for her to grab the fleeing slave and hold him. The overseer wanted Harriet to seize the boy and then help bind his hands so he could be whipped for his escape attempt.

Harriet not only refused to seize the boy—she deliberately blocked the path of the overseer. In a rage, the overseer picked up a heavy lead weight and hurled it at the runaway. The weight missed its mark and struck Harriet in the head. She fell to the ground unconscious. Harriet was carried back to her parents' cabin, where she remained in a coma for many days. She had sustained a dent in her head that remained all her life. She also began to suffer from "sleeping fits" and severe headaches. Harriet could not remain quiet for more than fifteen minutes before seeming to fall asleep. Even in sleep she was restless, and when awake she felt continually tired. The way she finally counteracted this malady was to do strenuous physical work in the direct heat of the sun. She felt this helped circulate her blood and improved her condition.[10]

After Harriet recovered somewhat from her head wound, she was directed to work for John Stewart, a shipbuilder. Harriet's father, Benjamin Ross, was already working for Stewart. Ross was an inspector who supervised a large crew, making sure their work was of high quality. Harriet was supposed to help Mrs. Stewart in the house, but she wanted to do outdoor work instead.

Soon Harriet was working alongside her father. She was about sixteen years old and she quickly grasped such tasks as cutting timber and driving oxen. It was said that Harriet was able to lift enormous barrels of produce and pull a heavily loaded boat.[11]

Harriet enjoyed the freedom of outdoor work because she was not under as close supervision as the house servants were.[12] When Harriet finished doing the work Stewart assigned, he allowed her to hire herself out for other logging jobs. She had to pay Stewart $50 from her wages, but anything over that was hers to keep. Harriet managed to save enough money to buy a team of oxen, and then she hired herself and the wagon out for hauling jobs. Harriet was only about five feet tall, but she was very muscular and could hold her own at men's jobs.

Harriet's parents raised their children with a strong faith in God. Harriet especially always felt the nearness of God, and she later told a friend that she talked to God "as a man talks with his friend."[13] Harriet had many visionary experiences. Some would occur during her sleeping spells. She would remember in detail what had happened while she seemed to be asleep. Harriet appears to have had mystical experiences all through her life, beginning in her teenage years. These directed her path and even warned her of dangers.[14]

While teenage Harriet was working alongside her father, dramatic events were shaking the region where she lived.

Nat Turner, a young Virginia slave who believed he had been chosen by God to overturn slavery, started a rebellion in 1831. Before being captured and killed, Turner and his companions killed fifty-one white people. This incident sent shock waves throughout the white South. Slave owners became even stricter because they were frightened of similar uprisings among their own slaves. There were hundreds of plots, escape attempts, and other signs of unrest among the slave population.

Harriet became aware of these incidents and also learned of the antislavery movement spreading in the United States. There were always white Americans disturbed by the institution of slavery, but now free blacks and sympathetic whites were joining forces to end slavery. This was called the abolition movement. Abolitionists spread the antislavery message by newspapers, speeches, pamphlets, and word of mouth.

The little girl who described herself as being "ignorant of liberty" began to learn about it. Working with her father to send logs to Baltimore, hiring herself out in places beyond Bucktown, Harriet came in contact with many different kinds of people. She learned from them what was happening in the wider world.

Harriet was unable to read or write because she had never been taught these skills, but she quickly grasped the idea of the human right of freedom. Although just a young girl, she sensed the justice in that runaway's flight to freedom the day she helped him and suffered a head injury.

Harriet realized there was something wrong in enslaving people and whipping them just because they had darker skin. Very soon Harriet would do something dramatic to grasp freedom for herself. She would become a beacon of hope to other slaves, a "Moses" helping to set her people free.

Chapter 3

LIBERTY OR DEATH

While Harriet Tubman was still a child, some slaves managed to escape from plantations in the South and flee to free states in the North. Most made the journey on their own. Many were caught and sent back to their masters, but some were able to find freedom.

In 1831, when Harriet was about eleven years old, people began using the term *Underground Railroad* to describe the pathways and way stations used by runaways in their flight to freedom. It was not a real railroad but a series of northward routes and houses or buildings along the way where the escaping slaves could take shelter. People who opposed slavery arranged for the secret places where the runaways could rest and get supplies.

The phrase Underground Railroad was used in 1831 when a slave named Tice Davids escaped from his Kentucky master. Davids's master pursued him to the edge of the Ohio River only to see him apparently vanish. The master cried out that Davids must have "gone off on an underground road."[1] And so a name was born to describe the many secret routes that led from southern plantations, across rivers and valleys, over mountains, all the way to the free North.

By the time Harriet was in her early twenties, thoughts of freedom were stirring in her heart, but she had not yet made plans to flee slavery by the Underground Railroad or any other means. She continued to work on the Brodas plantation and was also hired out for various other jobs. What she was thinking about was marriage. Most slave girls were "married" early, often in unions set up by their masters. Slaves were not permitted to marry under the law, so their marriages were common-law, informal arrangements. At twenty-four, Harriet was still single though. Then she met John Tubman.

A wealthy white man, Justice Richard Tubman, had come to Dorchester County in 1669 to claim one thousand acres he had received as a grant for fighting the Indians in many skirmishes. Richard Tubman owned many slaves, and they were all given his last name. The slaves worked in the family mansion and plantation on the western edge of Cambridge, Maryland, on the Choptank River. John Tubman's parents had been freed by their white master, so John was a free man. Of the eight thousand blacks in the area at the time, about half were free. Some, like Tubman, had been freed after their owners grew to oppose slavery. Other slaves were freed as a reward for long service and loyalty, and some bought their freedom.

John Tubman was literate and a free spirit. He seemed to have a measure of respect in the county. Harriet Ross and John Tubman began to court. They were married in 1844. Although Harriet was now the wife of a free man, she was not considered free. She was permitted to stay with her husband in his cabin at night, but her days and her labor still belonged to her white master. She was expected to report for work as usual at her master's house. Any children born to Harriet would be considered slaves and the property of the Brodas plantation. During this time children inherited the status of the mother: slave or free.

When Harriet Tubman was married, she looked into her own status. She had always heard rumors that her mother had been freed. If so, as a child of Harriet Greene Ross, she would be free, too. Using $5 of her precious savings, Harriet Tubman hired a lawyer to investigate her status. The lawyer went through sixty-five years of wills and other records. He discovered that Harriet Tubman's parents had indeed been freed upon the death of their original master. This happened before Harriet and her brothers and sisters were born, so the children had actually been born free. But the lawyer told Harriet Tubman that since she had always lived as a slave, no judge in Maryland would consider her free. This had a profound effect on Tubman. From then on she believed that she and her entire family were wrongly enslaved.[2]

Tubman continued to be a slave on the Brodas plantation and spent her nights with her husband. The selling of slaves increased on the plantation as the Brodas family finances declined further. The possibility of being sold to a cotton or rice plantation hung heavily over Harriet Tubman's head. The fact of her marriage would have no influence on whether or not she would be sold away from her husband. Breaking up families did not trouble the white owners.

Tubman prayed that her master would have a change of heart and would stop selling his slaves to southerners. "I was always praying," she later recalled, "Oh dear Lord change that man's heart."[3] When it became apparent to Tubman that her master would not change, she prayed that the Lord would take him out of the way so he could not do more mischief.[4]

Tubman lived with her husband for five years while working as a slave for the Brodas plantation. When Edward Brodas died, his slaves' fears about their futures grew. In March 1849, buyers came around with more frequency. Many were Georgia traders. Brodas's widow, Eliza Ann, needed money and she discussed trading Harriet Tubman and three of her brothers, who still lived on the plantation.

Harriet Tubman began having visions and hearing voices beckoning to her, "Arise, flee for your life!"[5] She talked with her husband about the visions and her anxieties about being sold. She told John Tubman that she wanted to run away. He was unsympathetic and even threatened to tell his wife's master that she was plotting to escape.[6]

At this time, any slaves who escaped and were recaptured were subject to brutal punishments. They could be whipped, have their ears cropped (the tops of their ears clipped off), or be branded with a hot iron. Anyone helping a slave escape was subject to five years' imprisonment. In 1849, the penalty was increased to fifteen years.

Harriet Tubman decided she must escape no matter what the dangers or the consequences. She knew very little about the North except that it was colder. She had vague notions of geography but no concept of maps at all. Tubman did know that the distance from Dorchester County to freedom in Pennsylvania was about one hundred miles. Going on foot, around hills, through swamps, skirting well-traveled roads and towns, it would be much farther.

The Choptank River, the largest river on the eastern shore of Maryland, ran northeast. Following the river would provide a reliable route. Tubman could rely on the North Star to guide her. She also knew how to read the clues of nature, such as the fact that moss grows thicker on the north side of trees.

Harriet spoke with her three brothers who still lived on the Brodas plantation. She told them of her plans to escape and hoped they might all leave together. Tubman longed to tell other friends and relatives, but she dared not for fear someone might accidentally betray her.[7]

One dark night, Tubman and her brothers walked away from the plantation. They walked eastward, following the Greenbriar Swamp, along the edge of the Brodas land to the hamlet of Bucktown. Tubman walked the familiar road singing softly, "Goodbye, I'm going to leave you. Goodbye, I'll meet you in the kingdom."[8] Nobody was alarmed because she often walked down that road singing. Even when she met Dr. Anthony Thompson, the clergyman who was managing the plantation for Mrs. Brodas, Tubman bowed toward him and sang all the louder.[9] Dr. Thompson later recalled how calm she had seemed, and how she appeared to be merely out for an evening stroll. "A wave of trouble never rolled across her peaceful breast," he marveled.[10]

Early into the journey, Harriet Tubman's brothers became frightened and turned back. She continued on alone. She was about twenty-nine years old, almost penniless, with nothing to rely on but her own courage and her dream of freedom.

Tubman hid by day and traveled by night. Her first stop was at the house of a white woman who had befriended her in the past while she worked at cutting and hauling wood. The woman quickly took Tubman into her cabin and gave her a meal. Then she gave Tubman two strips of paper, each containing the location of a safe house ahead and directions to reach it. In gratitude, Tubman gave the woman a patchwork quilt that was her only possession of any value. She had stitched the quilt after her marriage to John.

The next stop Tubman made was another cabin owned by some white people. She was promptly given a broom and told to start sweeping the front porch so she would look like an ordinary slave. Tubman did as she was told. If curious neighbors looked over, they would think the white family had a new servant. When night fell, a wagon pulled up to the cabin. It was half filled with vegetables. Tubman was told to climb in, cover herself with a cloth, and hide among the vegetables as the wagon rattled north.

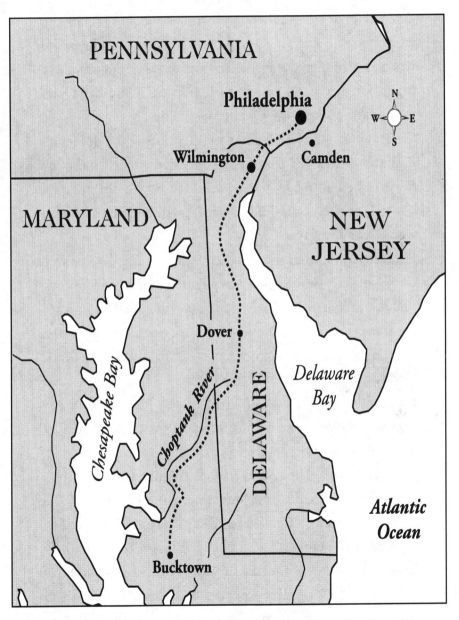

This map shows the route Harriet Tubman took to freedom, from Bucktown, Maryland, to Philadelphia, Pennsylvania (about 130 miles).

Tubman made the greater part of her journey north alone and on foot. There were times when sympathetic white people helped her along the way. Usually, though, she trudged through swamps and woodland with no shelter at night but woodland or potato holes, the board-lined pits where farmers kept their winter vegetables.

Tubman later recalled her feelings during the desperate flight. She reasoned that she would have either "liberty or death." She had made up her mind that if she did not gain her liberty she was willing to face death because "no man would take me slave."[11]

Harriet Tubman remained close to the Choptank River for about sixty-seven miles, keeping the North Star in front of her and to her left. She tried to stay off roads of any kind for fear of detection. The roads in Maryland were crowded with slave catchers who were eager to collect the cash rewards being offered for runaways. Tubman favored traveling through cemeteries, often spending nights there. She had no fear. She was comfortable with her belief in spirits and the supernatural.

Exhausted and footsore, Harriet Tubman finally reached Pennsylvania and crossed into freedom. She recalled the moment this way: "I had crossed the line of which I had so long been dreaming. I was free."[12] Tubman could scarcely believe that now, for the first time in her life, at almost thirty years old, she was a free woman. "I looked at my hands to see if I was the same person," she said. "There was such glory over everything. The sun came like gold through the trees." She said she felt as if she were "in heaven."[13]

Chapter 4

THE CONDUCTOR

arriet Tubman decided to go to Philadelphia to find work to support herself. She had saved some money from being hired out while she was enslaved, but it would not be enough to sustain her for long. She had been working since she was six years old and she knew how to do many jobs. Tubman had been a housekeeper, a nanny, a cook, and a skilled outdoor laborer. She did not think she would have much trouble getting employment, and she was right. She quickly got a job as a cook in a hotel, earning $1 a day.

Tubman rented a small room near her job. As she earned money, she furnished her quarters. She did not spend much money, even on necessities, because she wanted to save as much as possible.

Although Tubman was now free, she was very lonely and she longed for the faces of family and friends back home. When she came to Philadelphia, she knew no one to welcome her there. "I was a stranger in a strange land," she later said of her arrival.[1] The friends she made in Philadelphia were kind, but she had left so many loved ones behind, still in slavery.

In 1850, Tubman visited the Philadelphia Vigilance Committee offices. This was the main eastern station for the Underground Railroad. William Still, a black man, was in charge of the organization. It offered assistance, day or night, to fugitive slaves. Here Tubman learned all about the Railroad and how widespread it was. Runaways received food and clothing, help in getting jobs, loans of money, and information about families back home.

There are no written records of most of the activities of runaway slaves. The majority of the slaves were illiterate and those who helped them were too busy to keep records. Also, runaway slaves and their sympathizers feared that leaving records would increase the chances of being caught and returned to slavery. But William Still did keep extensive records of the fugitives who passed through his station. He believed these were necessary to reunite families and let loved ones know what happened to their kinfolk who seemed one night to drop off the earth without a trace.

Still kept careful records of runaways' names, how many were in each party, physical descriptions, names of masters they had run from, the county where they had lived, and the date of their arrival in Philadelphia. Because the discovery of these records would have been a disaster, he kept them hidden in a graveyard, and none were ever found by slave catchers. Eventually, after slavery was abolished, Still gathered all these records, notes, and letters into a book titled *Underground Railroad*. The eight-hundred-page book narrates the hardships, narrow escapes, and amazing courage of many runaways and the people who helped them.

Almost every night, after a day of cooking and cleaning in the hotel, Tubman climbed the steep wooden steps to the loft to meet with Still and others. Tubman was eager to play a role in helping more slaves escape. She believed that the whole system of slavery was evil and had to be stopped. Not only was it miserable for the slaves, she thought, it was even bad for their masters.[2] Tubman once called slavery "the next thing to hell."[3]

Tubman wanted to bring her own family to freedom. "I was free and they should be free also," she later said.[4] She dreamed of bringing them all to Philadelphia, but she did not know how to go about it. Still, from that time forward, she dedicated her life to the cause of freeing the slaves.

On a visit to the Vigilance Committee, Tubman learned of a black woman about to be sold away from her family in Maryland. She was shocked to discover that it was her own sister, Mary. Tubman struggled to keep track of all her siblings, but once they were sold away or married, she had no way to communicate with them.

Tubman's sister was Mary Bowley, the wife of a free black man, John Bowley. They had two children who were going to be sold along with their mother. Tubman's rescue of the

Bowley family would be her first experience as a "conductor" on the Underground Railroad.

Mary Bowley and her children had already been taken from the plantation. They awaited buyers in the slave pen in Cambridge, Maryland, where an auction of a large number of slaves was to be held. Buyers from all over the South would be bidding for the slaves.

Tubman's plan was for John Bowley to pose as an agent for the auctioneer. He was to go to the slave pen and request custody of Mary Bowley and the children on the pretense that a buyer was waiting in the hotel to inspect them more closely.

Mary and the children were turned over to John Bowley, and the little family marched down the street toward the hotel. It looked as if a slave was bringing new slaves to his master for evaluation—but it was really the escape of a family.

John Bowley hustled his wife and children into a house owned by a Quaker (a member of the religious group the Society of Friends) who was sympathetic to fugitive slaves. They remained there until nightfall, when, under cover of darkness, a wagon rolled up to the house. The Bowley family piled in and was covered with blankets. Then the wagon rattled off toward the river. At the river, the four climbed into a boat Tubman had hired, and they headed for Baltimore. They were told to keep watch for two lights on the opposite shore, one yellow, one blue. The lights would be hung from barns, and when the Bowleys saw them they would know the coast was clear. Finally they saw the lights and hurried toward a wagon parked along the road.

A white woman sat bent over on the wagon seat. The wagon was loaded with potatoes and onions, and the Bowleys crawled among the vegetables on the bouncy ride to a house in Baltimore. They remained hiding there for a week until Harriet Tubman arrived to take them to Philadelphia. She had planned every detail of the escape, hiring the wagons and arranging for the safe houses. Now, with the help of the Philadelphia Vigilance Committee, Tubman found the Bowleys housing and jobs. Tubman's first experience as a conductor was successful because of careful planning, but her future rescues would be much more hazardous.

In 1851, Tubman returned to Maryland to help one of her brothers, John Ross, escape. He was working in Talbot County, just north of Dorchester County. After Tubman arranged her brother's escape, her thoughts turned to her husband. She had not seen him in two years. Tubman hoped she might persuade John to join her in Philadelphia, where they could resume their married life. John Tubman did not appear to love Harriet as much as she loved him.[5] He was a free man, and it would have been easy for him to move north and join his wife if he wanted to.

Harriet Tubman saved her wages for a long time until she finally had enough to make the trip back to Dorchester County, Maryland, to visit her husband. She brought him a brand-new suit from a men's store in Philadelphia as a gift.

She was still considered a fugitive slave, so Harriet Tubman could not travel openly. She set out in disguise, again traveling by night and using safe houses to rest in. When she arrived near her husband's cabin, friends approached her with surprising news. They said John Tubman had taken a new wife, a woman named Caroline. Harriet did not go directly to the cabin to confront her husband or the woman who had taken her place. Instead she sent a friend with a message that she was now living in Philadelphia and wanted her husband to join her there.

John Tubman sent back his answer at once. He was very happy with his new wife and had no desire to live with Harriet again. She was awash in grief and anger.[6] She considered going to her husband's cabin despite the danger that she might be captured. She told her friends that she wanted to "see [her] old man once more."[7] Common sense prevailed, and Harriet decided that if John could do without her, then she could do without him, too.[8] Later she said that at that moment, John Tubman "dropped out of" her heart.[9]

The Tubmans never saw each other again. In spite of the breakup of her marriage, Harriet Tubman continued to use her husband's last name.

Harriet Tubman now committed herself even more wholeheartedly to the cause of fugitive slaves. The Fugitive Slave Act in the 1850 Compromise made Tubman's cause even more dangerous. Runaway slaves could be captured in the North and returned to their owners in the South even before the passage of this law, but now federal officials had the right and duty to return runaway slaves to their owners.

Anyone interfering with this activity was subject to heavy penalties.

Tubman and the other conductors on the Underground Railroad now had more to do than merely get their charges over the Mason-Dixon line into freedom. Slaves were no longer safe even after they reached the North. With bounties on their heads, they could be seized at any time and dragged back to slavery in chains.

The only true safety now lay even farther north, in Canada.

Chapter 5

LET MY PEOPLE GO

In 1851, Harriet Tubman visited Canada for the first
time. Because she would be bringing escaping slaves
there, she had to survey the terrain and discover what
problems they might encounter. Entering Canada would
require the fugitives to cross the bridge suspended over
Niagara Falls. It would be a frightening experience for these
people to hear the roar of the falls and walk through the spray
of the crashing water.

Tubman began to work out every detail of the journey.
In each small town north of Maryland, she arranged for safe
houses. In the Cooper house in Camden, New Jersey, she
would conceal her charges in a small, bunk-lined room
above the kitchen. In Odessa, Delaware, they would stay in

a loft under a pitched roof in a Quaker meetinghouse. All this Tubman took pains to remember. She did not—could not—write anything down.

Tubman often described a vision she had as a young girl. The vision almost haunted her with its frequency. She saw a line dividing freedom from slavery. On the northern side stood people stretching out their hands in welcome, bidding Tubman to come forward, calling her "Moses."[1] She kept that vision in her mind as she planned her rescues.

Tubman had a fine memory, and she would later recount the details of her many trips south to rescue slaves. But the only written record of her activities is contained in William Still's records.

Still recorded six of Tubman's groups of runaways and mentioned others in fragmentary ways. His first entry mentioning Tubman as a conductor is dated December 29, 1854. Tubman had brought six men and one woman to freedom. During the long walk, Tubman and one of the men had worn the shoes off their feet. Still's notes describe a twenty-year-old named John who had fled a master he called "a hard man." Twenty-eight-year-old Benjamin had escaped a "very devilish" mistress. Twenty-two-year-old Jane called her master, Rash Jones, "the worst man in the country." The others had similar stories of being worked hard and treated, as thirty-five-year-old Robert recalled, like a "dumb brute."[2]

Tubman always varied her route. She wanted to confuse any slave catchers who might be on her trail. Sometimes she used the mountains and sometimes she followed the trail from Cambridge, Maryland, over the Choptank River bridges to the towns in Delaware.

It was not easy to elude the bloodhounds that were often sent to find runaway slaves. The owners of the bloodhounds charged $5 a day for hunting the trails. The dogs trained for hunting slaves were valuable. A pack of ten bloodhounds was sold in Columbia, South Carolina, for $1,540. These dogs could take a three-day-old scent and track it down, and they were said to be swifter than greyhounds when they were on the run.[3] The slave catchers earned bounties ranging from several hundred dollars to many thousands for a valuable slave.

When Tubman went south to contact slaves who wanted to flee, she would softly sing verses from spirituals as she moved along the plantation boundaries. The hymn "Go Down Moses," which was heard in the South during the mid-1800s, had a special connection with Tubman's exploits.[4] Some of the lyrics are:

"Go down, Moses, way down in Egypt's land;
Tell old Pharaoh, to let my people go."[5]

It was sung by Tubman and by many of the conductors who led slaves to freedom. Word would be whispered from slave to slave that Moses was in the area ready to shepherd another party north. The words of the spirituals were understood by the slaves, but not by their masters. They were coded messages that could be safely sung without alerting the masters or overseers of escape plans. "Egypt" meant the South, and "Pharaoh" stood for the slave owners.

The "Israelites" were the slaves, and "Canaan land" was Canada. The Jordan River, which was mentioned in many spirituals, including other stanzas of "Go Down Moses," was the point of departure for the runaways.[6] Sometimes the code involved singing a verse twice, followed by silence. This meant the coast was clear and the escape plan could proceed.[7]

The ideal time for escaping a plantation was on a Saturday night. Often a slave would not be missed until Monday morning, when work began again. Sometimes a white person spotted Tubman as she lingered in the woods waiting for the runaway. Tubman knew just what to do. She acted like a humble slave, bowing and scraping before the white person. She did not seem like someone to be suspected of rebellious activity. The white observer would invariably leave her alone, and once again "Moses" would escape.[8]

The slaves Tubman was spiriting away were often worth hundreds or even thousands of dollars. Their loss represented a real financial blow to the plantations. Their owners were very anxious to get them back, and they would send men north to nail posters to trees and fence posts offering rewards for the slaves' return. Tubman had a strategy for this, too. She would hire a man to secretly follow the men putting up the posters. He would remain at a safe distance, then he would simply tear the posters down.

Tubman was soon legendary among the slaves. Even those far from Maryland knew about her. She was an inspiration to slaves all over the South. Thomas Cole, a slave from Huntsville, Alabama, said that during his own escape he kept hoping and praying he might meet up with that "Harriet Tubman woman."[9]

A $10,000 reward was offered for the capture of Harriet Tubman. Later, the reward was increased to $40,000.[10] Tubman was not concerned by this. She believed she was invincible. "The whites cannot catch us for I was born with the charm, and the Lord has given me the power," she said.[11]

Between 1851 and 1857, Tubman usually made two trips a year to the eastern shore of Maryland, one in the spring and one in the fall. She conducted her passengers north using safe houses when they were available and making do when they were not. Tubman hid her charges in drainage ditches, abandoned sheds, and barns. Once, Tubman and her group hid in a manure pile.

Tubman made many friends, both black and white, during her Underground Railroad exploits. One of them was Thomas Garrett, a Quaker from Wilmington, Delaware, who ran a large shoe store. When fugitives came through town, he always made sure they were fitted with a new pair of shoes before they continued their journey. Garrett also hid runaway slaves in a false wall in his shoe store. Garrett and Tubman often worked together, and he held her in high esteem. "No slave who placed himself under her care was ever arrested that I have heard of," Garrett said.[12]

Tubman told Garrett, as she told all her friends, that God played a major role in her ability to rescue slaves. She said that sometimes, as she led a group of fugitives, she would hear the voice of God telling her to stop where she was. She would obey the voice and await further instructions.

Garrett said that Tubman never had the slightest doubt that the voices she heard were from God and that they would lead her in the right direction. Jokingly, Garrett once asked Tubman if God had ever deceived her. She answered with a resounding "No!"[13] Garrett was so impressed with Tubman's unshakable faith and the success of all her missions that he concluded that there was indeed "something remarkable" involved.[14]

Tubman told Garrett a story about leading a group of fugitives through a field on a cold day in March. She believed that God was telling her to cross a chilly river where there was no bridge. It would be necessary to wade through the cold water. The men in the party were afraid to cross, and they hesitated to follow Tubman's orders to wade into the water. Tubman led the way, entering the water until it reached her armpits and proceeding to walk through the river to the opposite shore. When they saw that this small woman had made it, the others followed, but they had no idea where they were going. They clambered to dry land on the opposite shore, soaking wet and trembling with the cold. All they had to lean on was Tubman and her voices from God.[15]

The other side of the river looked like a thick wilderness, offering no food or shelter. Then, as they walked, they made out the form of a small cabin. As they neared the cabin, they found it was occupied by a black family, who generously took the whole group in. The family gave the fugitives food, dried their clothing, and provided shelter. Tubman had no money with which to repay the family for such kindness, so she gave them some items of her own clothing in thanks.

Garrett and Tubman together were able to help many fugitive slaves. Garrett also helped hundreds of slaves to freedom on his own, and for this he paid heavily. He was twice arrested for aiding runaways and was fined so heavily that he had to sell everything he owned, including his shoe store. At sixty years of age, he was penniless and was forced to take any job he could find just to support himself and his family. But even then he continued to work with Tubman in the Underground Railroad. When he was arrested again, the large fine left him totally destitute. The judge told Garrett that this harsh lesson ought to teach him to never again be "helping off runaway Negroes."[16] Garrett responded by saying that the court had taken his last dollar, but he would never stop befriending the fugitives as long as one of them needed his help.[17]

Nothing could stop Harriet Tubman either, not even her many close calls.

Chapter 6

YOU WILL BE FREE OR DIE

O ne of Harriet Tubman's many close encounters with disaster occurred as she led a group of fugitives on a wild, rainy night. She headed for the home of a black ally she had often relied on. His home was a safe house on the Underground Railroad. She wanted food and dry lodging for her wet band of runaways, so she left them huddled in the street near the cabin and rapped on the door in the usual way. Tubman used a special tapping signal that other agents of the Railroad recognized. When nobody inside the cabin responded, Tubman repeated the signal. Then a white face appeared, not the black one she had expected. The irate white man demanded to know who this black woman was—and why she was pounding on his door in the middle of the night.

Tubman asked about the black family that used to live in this cabin, and the new white owner snapped that they were long gone. They had been driven off, he said, for "harboring" slaves.[1]

When one of the safe houses along the Underground Railroad was exposed, it was abandoned quickly, but word had not reached Tubman in time. It was sometimes impossible to warn the groups of fugitives making their way through field and swamp that their safe house had been closed down. That is why Tubman had approached the house alone, ordering her charges to wait in hiding. She was never sure what she would find.

Tubman hurried back to her little band of frightened runaways shivering in the rain. Then she closed her eyes and listened to her inner guide voice. The voice told her to take the group outside town to a little island that rose from a swamp. Tubman took them there and told them to lie down in the tall, wet grass while she prayed for deliverance. Everyone was terrified and chilled to the bone as Tubman implored heaven for help. Tubman refused to let anyone leave the island because she now believed help would find them there.

The group had been there for several hours when a stranger came walking to the edge of the swamp. Tubman had never seen him before. He was a white man dressed like a Quaker—in dark, undecorated garb. The man began speaking as if to himself. He said that his wagon stood by his farmhouse and the horse's harness was hanging on a nail. His horse was also in the stable. After the man said all this, he walked away.

Harriet led the fugitives to the farmhouse, where they found everything the man had described. The wagon was well provisioned for their journey, and the group piled in to continue the journey. Tubman was not the least bit surprised by such an unusual deliverance. It did not strike her as strange or mysterious at all. She prayed and she fully expected her prayers to be answered.[2]

Whenever it appeared that Tubman and her parties were close to being captured, she escaped by using her quick wits as well as the warnings she believed she received from heaven.[3] Tubman sensed when danger was near. She said later that when slave catchers were in the area, her heart went "flutter, flutter."[4] Through prayers, dreams, and waking visions she was able to foresee danger, devise a strategy to escape, and remain free with those she guided.[5]

It was understood that once a slave decided to run away from the plantation and join Harriet Tubman's group, there was no turning back. The runaway was committed to remain with the group no matter what. If, in a moment of fear or weakness, a fugitive wanted to turn back and return to the plantation, Tubman would not allow it.

Tubman kept a revolver to help convince timid souls not to go back. A slave who had been on the Underground Railroad and then returned to the plantation could be frightened or tortured into betraying Tubman's secrets. The whole network of safe houses, agents, and white and black allies who made the Railroad possible would be put in danger. Showing her revolver to a faltering soul she would say, "You'll be free or die."[6] In Pennsylvania, troopers were raiding the homes of whites when those known to be against slavery were suspected of aiding fugitives.[7]

Tubman believed that if a fugitive was weak enough to change his mind about escaping, he would be weak enough to betray everyone who had helped him along the way. "Do you think I'd let so many die just for one coward man?" she asked.[8] On one occasion a member of Tubman's party had feet so sore and swollen that he pleaded to be left behind. Tubman turned to the other men in the party and told them to get their guns ready because this man needed to be shot rather than left behind to betray them. Tubman recalled that when the man with the sore feet heard that, he jumped right up and continued the journey with a step as good as the rest.[9]

Tubman was tough when she needed to be, and it worked. She often said, "I never ran my train off the track and I never lost a passenger."[10]

In late 1854, Harriet Tubman became troubled about the fate of her brothers back in Maryland.[11] She heard rumors that right after Christmas her three brothers were going to be sold south to a rice or cotton plantation. Christmas was a rare time of feasting and relaxation for the slaves, so the deed was being postponed until after the holidays.

When Tubman heard of the pending sale, she swung into action. When she had first fled slavery, she had tried to convince her brothers to flee with her. Her first rescue was of her sister, Mary, and her family. Now Tubman resolved to bring the three brothers at last to freedom.

Tubman arrived at the Brodas plantation, which was still owned by Eliza Ann Brodas, on Christmas Eve and spirited her three brothers away. The four of them went to the small cabin where their parents, Benjamin and Rit, lived. Tubman and her brothers did not show themselves to their parents but instead hid in the outbuildings behind the cabin. All night they hid in sheds and in the cornstalks near the cabin. As much as Tubman longed to talk with her parents, she dared not show her face. She feared that when her brothers were found missing, the overseer would come to their parents' cabin and question the old people about their children. Tubman wanted her parents to be able to say honestly that they had not set eyes on their daughter in a long time, nor seen their sons since they vanished from the plantation.

The cabin where Benjamin and Rit lived was about forty miles from the Brodas plantation. Usually the old folks were visited by any of their children in the area at Christmas. But this year, because of the need for secrecy, they would pass this Christmas alone, not knowing that one of their daughters and three of their sons were hiding only yards away.

One of Tubman's brothers had a wife and a child, with a second child on the way. On Christmas Eve, the woman went into labor and was in no condition to travel. But the party had to leave by dawn, so the wife and two children were left behind. There is no record of what happened to them.

Before dawn, according to the plan, Tubman led her three brothers, and those members of their families who were strong enough to travel by foot, on a hundred-mile journey. They arrived in Wilmington, Delaware, and were given refuge by Thomas Garrett until their passage to Canada could be arranged. Eventually they all arrived safely in Canada.

In another daring rescue during the mid-1850s, Tubman had to venture near her master's home to contact a slave who wanted to escape. Tubman was a master of disguise and she was especially good at appearing to be an old, frail woman with a halting gait. This time she wrapped herself in a shawl and walked bent over as though she were crippled. For good measure she brought two live chickens, which she carried by a cord around their feet. If someone who knew her appeared, she would need to cause a distraction. When she saw her master's son approaching, she freed the startled chickens and they flew into the air squawking noisily. The young man might have recognized Tubman, but he was so startled that he never took a good look at the black woman and she hurried safely by.

Sometimes Tubman gave groups of fugitives directions north. If they seemed capable, they went alone. In other cases, when Tubman sensed that the group was frightened or unsure, she accompanied them every step of the way to freedom.

To finance her trips south and to get money for the destitute slaves she rescued, Tubman sought money and supplies from her white friends in various northern cities.

Tubman had support in Philadelphia and Boston because strong antislavery groups existed there and they knew of the Underground Railroad. Most of the runaway slaves arrived in rags, walking on bare, bloodied feet. Often their skills were limited to plantation labor, which did not translate easily into jobs in the North. They desperately needed money to tide them over in their new home, and Tubman tried to provide as much as she could.

Harriet Tubman's fame was spreading beyond the United States through antislavery activists visiting friends in Europe. A few donations even arrived from Europe earmarked for Tubman's work. The funds were sent in care of Thomas Garrett.

One day in 1857, Tubman was desperately in need of money to return to the eastern shore of Maryland to bring more fugitives out. She needed clothing and shoes for herself and her charges. Tubman visited Garrett and told him she had a dream that he had money for her. Only a day earlier, Garrett had indeed received a donation from an antislavery sympathizer in Scotland. In the letter were five English pounds. The money met all Tubman's immediate needs, with nothing left over. She quickly left for Maryland, confident again that whatever she needed would be provided.

The journey Tubman took when leading groups to Canada extended from Rochester, New York, to the town of Saint Catharines in Canada. On the south shore of Lake Ontario, with a population of six thousand, including about seven hundred blacks, Saint Catharines was a port city with a telegraph line and neat wooden houses for its residents.

There were about thirty thousand black Americans living in the general area, many of them fugitive slaves. In 1833, slavery had been forbidden in all of the British Empire, including Canada.

The former slaves who came to Canada had to contend with very harsh winters, bitterly cold and snowy. This was especially hard on slaves who had lived in the Deep South. Adjusting to the many differences between the South and the North was difficult for all the fugitives. Soon after arriving in Canada, some of the fugitives took jobs cutting wood in the forests. Others worked in hotels or homes.

American slaveholder and politician Henry Clay said that blacks fleeing to Canada were worthless, and he advised, "the sooner they are gotten rid of, the better for Canada."[12] Canadians, however, did not share Clay's negative view of their new residents. Blacks were treated cordially and without prejudice. They were allowed to buy tracts of land for the going rate of $2 an acre for fifty-acre tracts. The cost could be paid over ten years. Many former slaves became successful farmers in Canada. The Anti-Slavery Society of Canada reported in 1853 that all the former slaves required was "a fair chance, friendly advice, and a little encouragement, perhaps a little assistance at first."[13]

In 1857, Harriet Tubman began to worry very much about her parents. She had tried to get the elderly couple out of Maryland before, but they did not want to go. Many of their relatives and friends still lived nearby, and at this stage in their lives Tubman's parents feared being uprooted from familiar surroundings. But Tubman had, by now, brought her brother, a sister, and the three brothers who lived in Maryland north to freedom. Tubman's parents had lost track of other children who had long been sold away. Harriet Tubman feared that her parents would soon be left alone without children nearby. Tubman's parents were frail and Tubman worried what would become of them when they could no longer care for themselves.

It was the courage of Harriet Tubman's father that brought matters to a head. Old Benjamin Ross had been helping other slaves escape, and now he was in trouble. He had been ordered to appear in court to face charges. That was all Tubman needed to hear to spring into action. She got some money from the Anti-Slavery Society and headed for Maryland to bring her parents to freedom.

Chapter 7

THE LAST DAYS OF
THE RAILROAD

Benjamin Ross, about seventy years old, was facing legal action for helping to free a fellow slave. With his trial looming, Harriet Tubman headed south. She worried about the obstacles that lay ahead. The slaves she helped were generally young and strong. The three-hundred-mile journey from Maryland to Canada was challenging enough for the able-bodied young, but how could her old parents survive the arduous trip? They could scarcely walk many miles from their cabin. How could they be expected to walk the hundreds of miles through swamp and field? Clearly, a different approach would be necessary.

Tubman had some money with her, borrowed from her friends at the Anti-Slavery Society, but she did not have

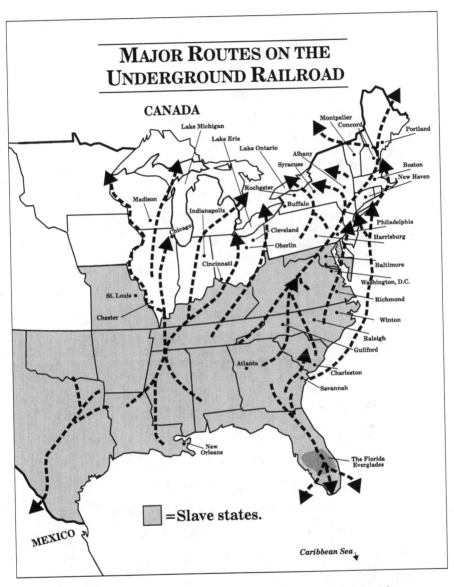

MAJOR ROUTES ON THE UNDERGROUND RAILROAD

CANADA

Montpelier
Concord
Portland
Lake Michigan
Lake Erie
Lake Ontario
Albany
Syracuse
Boston
New Haven
Rochester
Madison
Buffalo
Indianapolis
Chicago
Philadelphia
Cleveland
Harrisburg
Oberlin
Cincinnati
Baltimore
Washington, D.C.
St. Louis
Richmond
Chester
Winton
Raleigh
Guilford
Atlanta
Charleston
Savannah
New Orleans
The Florida Everglades
☐ =Slave states.
MEXICO
Caribbean Sea

The Underground Railroad extended all the way to Canada. There, slaves were at last free from the risk of being captured and returned to their masters. (Some slaves instead fled to Mexico, Florida, and the Caribbean.)

much. When she arrived in Caroline County, where her parents lived, she bought an old horse and a pair of wheels on an axle. She laid a board across the axle for a seat and hung a second board from the axle for a footrest. Then she hitched the horse to this makeshift buggy with a rope and straw collar. Tubman told her parents they were going to freedom.

Benjamin Ross agreed to go, but not without his broadax and other tools. Rit Ross insisted on bringing her feather bedtick. Harriet Tubman loaded all these possessions on the makeshift wagon and helped her parents aboard.[1] Tubman drove the strange-looking vehicle as the journey began in the dead of night.[2] They drove for many miles until they were far from home. Then Harriet Tubman gave her parents forged passes and put them on a train to Wilmington, Delaware. Tubman drove on alone to Wilmington and met her parents there at Thomas Garrett's home.

Before Tubman took her parents to Canada, they visited with William Still in Philadelphia and he had a long talk with the old couple. Benjamin Ross described his master, Dr. Anthony Thompson, as a "wolf in sheep's clothing," who allowed the Rosses little food and clothing, made them live in rough conditions, and had not even given them a dollar for the past twenty years. When Benjamin and Rit Ross remembered the "portion of their children" who had been sold away to slavery in Georgia, Still noted that they spoke with "much feeling."[3]

Harriet Tubman had her headquarters in Saint Catharines, where she lived while arranging for the arrival of fugitives. She boarded a railroad car with her parents and set off for Canada, arriving there in the middle of winter. Tubman settled her parents in a little house. That first winter in the north was very difficult for the old couple. The bone-chilling cold made them ill. Harriet Tubman had to work very hard doing chores for the local farmers to support her parents. While they were slaves, the Rosses had received meager provisions from their master, but now they had nothing at all but what their daughter provided. Tubman chopped wood in the snowy forest and sold the logs for firewood to the farmers, barely earning enough money to provide food for her parents.

At about this time, one of Tubman's friends, William Seward, then the governor of New York, came to the rescue. He knew of a parcel of land for sale in his hometown of Auburn, New York. He thought it might make a perfect home for Tubman and her parents. Auburn was a friendly place, a center of antislavery sentiment and support for woman suffrage—the right of women to vote. Seward asked Tubman how much money she could gather, and when the property was auctioned, he made sure that Tubman's bid was accepted. Tubman was able to make the down payment and Seward arranged small monthly payments for the balance.

Getting a house of her own was a godsend for Tubman, especially when her parents were suffering so much from the Canadian cold weather. Tubman brought her parents down to Auburn and settled them in the sturdy little house. They would spend the rest of their lives there. This was also to be Tubman's home for the balance of her life, though she would often be away on her Underground Railroad duties and later as a participant in the Civil War. She was gone for long periods of time, but she could rely on friends in Auburn to look after her parents.

During the late 1850s, in addition to her work rescuing slaves, Harriet Tubman began to speak at New England antislavery meetings and at other public forums. She was a much-sought-after speaker with her harrowing tales of narrow escapes. She was never paid for her appearances, as other famous African Americans—Sojourner Truth and Frederick Douglass—were, but she frequented conventions, lectures, picnics, and fairs, and she was never shy about talking about her experiences.

On July 4, 1859, in Farmingham, Massachusetts, Tubman was introduced to the audience by Thomas Higginson, president of the Massachusetts Anti Slavery Society. In August 1859, she spoke to the New England Colored Citizens Convention. She told her audience that she disliked the idea favored by some well-meaning people urging blacks to leave the United States and return to Africa.

When she spoke, Tubman would mount the speaker's platform, smiling though her upper front teeth were gone. She wore coarse but neat clothing and always carried a small net bag.[4] A reporter in 1859 said she spoke in a style of "quaint simplicity."[5] Though uneducated, she had real eloquence, a well-stocked mind, and a remarkable memory. She had never read the Bible, but she had heard passages spoken and she could recite them from memory.[6]

Tubman made friends with many famous people of her day who shared her sentiments about slavery. She knew Susan B. Anthony, the suffragist. Anthony helped Tubman clothe some fugitive slave women who arrived in the North in tatters.[7] When Tubman was in Concord, Massachusetts, she lodged at the home of the writer Ralph Waldo Emerson, or at the home of Mrs. Horace Mann, widow of the famous educator. Sometimes Tubman stayed with the Alcotts. (Louisa May Alcott is best remembered as the author of *Little Women* and *Little Men*.) Other famous people who maintained a warm friendship with Harriet Tubman were William Lloyd Garrison, publisher of the antislavery newspaper *The Liberator*, Charles Sumner, the fiery Massachusetts senator who fought slavery, and Governor Andrew of Massachusetts. All these famous people admired the work Tubman was doing.[8]

Once, Harriet Tubman had a vivid dream in which she imagined she was viewing a great wilderness. Suddenly a snake raised its head among the rocks. As Tubman stared at the snake, it changed into the head of an old white man with a long white beard and snow-white hair. Then two other heads appeared, both of them younger white men. They surrounded the old man, then rushed in and struck him. The old man stared at Tubman with a forlorn "wishful" look, Tubman said.[9] Tubman did not understand the significance of the strange dream until the spring of 1858, when a fervent antislavery activist named John Brown visited her at Saint Catharines.

John Brown had heard of Tubman's bravery in the Underground Railroad and her soldier-like qualities. Brown wanted to get a prominent black person on board for his planned slave uprising. When Tubman met him, she recognized his face from the vivid dreams. He was the old man transformed from the snake's head.

John Brown was impressed with Harriet, and he began calling her General Tubman.[10] He shared with her his plans to invade Virginia. He wanted her to recruit slaves for a general uprising after he captured the government arsenal at Harpers Ferry.

John Brown had a violent past. He was involved in the Underground Railroad in Pennsylvania, but then he joined up with antislavery forces in Kansas. When pro-slavery activists burned the town of Lawrence, Kansas, Brown and his sons struck back by killing slavery supporters at Pottawatamie Creek in 1856. From then on, his name was associated with violent resistance to slavery.

Tubman was in agreement with Brown's plan to raid Harpers Ferry in Virginia and cause a general slave uprising there. Tubman was so impressed with Brown that later she rated him as a greater man than President Abraham Lincoln.[11] Tubman waited for Brown's instructions, but she did not stand idle. In the spring of 1859 she was involved in a wild incident to save an escaped slave who was about to be returned to his master.

Charles Nalle, a fugitive slave, was handcuffed and led from the United States Marshal's office in Troy, New York. An unusual twist in the story is that Nalle was half white and looked like a white man. Still, he was a slave because he had a slave parent.

In the crowd of onlookers that day was Harriet Tubman. When Nalle appeared, Tubman shouted to her friends, "Here he comes—take him!"[12] Tubman seized one officer who was holding Nalle, and she pulled him down. Then she pulled the other officer away, and she wrapped her arms around Nalle and cried, "Don't let them have him!"[13]

In the melee that followed, Tubman removed her sunbonnet and tied it on Nalle's head to confuse the lawmen. She hoped they could not pick Nalle out among the sea of people.

As Tubman and her friends pulled Nalle along, they were frequently knocked down. Nalle himself, still handcuffed, was bleeding from the violent jostling. Tubman's outer clothing was torn from her body, and her shoes were ripped from her feet, but she continued, barefoot, refusing to release her hold on Nalle.

The mob reached the river and Nalle was shoved into a boat. Tubman jumped into another boat to follow him. But the lawmen used the telegraph to notify officials on the other shore, and the moment Nalle landed, a swarm of lawmen seized him. Nalle was taken to a house to be held until his master could come for him.

But Tubman did not give up her struggle. She and her friends raced up the stairs of the house, burst into the room where Nalle was being held, and dragged him out, carrying him down the stairs.

When Tubman and her allies reached the street, a sympathetic wagon driver took pity on them. He offered his wagon, pulled by a swift horse, for the escape. Tubman and the others carried Nalle off to safety in Schenectady, New York. During her valiant struggle for one man's freedom, Tubman was repeatedly beaten over the head. She never doubted whether the struggle was worth the cost, however, for another fugitive slave was free. Later, Nalle settled in Washington, D.C., and raised a brood of red-headed children.

In the fall of 1859, the call finally came from John Brown. He was ready to implement his plan to attack Harpers Ferry, and he tried to reach Harriet Tubman at her home in Canada, asking her to join him. Brown then learned that Tubman had moved to Auburn, New York, and he contacted her there. But Tubman had been traveling and was ill from exhaustion. She was lying very sick at a friend's house in New Bedford, Massachusetts. Only her illness kept her from going to Virginia to be at John Brown's side.[14]

John Brown went ahead with his plans without Tubman. On October 16, 1859, he and twenty-one men attacked the Harpers Ferry arsenal. A company of United States marines and soldiers led by Colonel Robert E. Lee was sent to put down the attack and capture John Brown and his men. After a fierce battle, two of Brown's sons were killed, along with eight other men. Brown himself was captured. He was put on trial for murder and treason and hanged on December 2, 1859.

Harriet Tubman grieved for her friend John Brown. After his death she was visiting a friend's home in Concord, Massachusetts, where she was shown a bust of Brown. The sight of it sent her into a spell of deep sorrow.[15] When Brown died, Harriet Tubman finally understood the meaning of that strange dream of the old white man struck down in the wilderness.

On December 1, 1860, Harriet Tubman made her last trip on the Underground Railroad. She brought out Stephen Ennets, his wife, Maris, six-year-old Harriet, four-year-old Amanda, and a three-month-old baby. Tubman had to use paregoric, a sedative, to quiet the baby when the child's crying imperiled the party. Tubman got the Ennets family safely to Canada.

On April 12, 1861, the federal garrison at Fort Sumter, South Carolina, was fired on by southern guns. The Civil War was under way and Harriet Tubman's life would change drastically. During the war she would serve her people and her country in a new and dangerous way.

Chapter 8

SCOUT, SPY, NURSE, SOLDIER

As war broke out between the North and South in 1861, Harriet Tubman recalled a vision she had in 1857. She was visiting the Reverend Henry Highland Garnet in New York when she dreamed that all black people in the United States were free. She awoke singing, "My people are free!"[1] Garnet, who was also black, scolded her. He warned her that they would never see freedom for black people in their lifetimes. But perhaps their grandchildren would see it, he thought. Tubman replied, "You'll see it and you'll see it soon."[2]

Harriet Tubman hoped that President Abraham Lincoln would free the slaves at once, but that did not happen. She believed that God would not let Lincoln win the war until he had set the slaves free.[3]

With the war under way, the slaves had new problems. As plantations were overrun with Union troops, the slaves scattered. Without any means of support, they were a vast group of hungry, homeless, desperate people.

The displaced slaves who milled about the roads were called "contraband." Tubman learned that the government needed help to deal with them. The slaves no longer had masters, but still they were not free. The contraband had no shelter or food. They were malnourished, cold, and wet, and many were sick. Thousands of men, women, and children clogged the roads. The very force of their numbers prevented some units of the Union Army from functioning.

A white soldier recalled a group of slaves who approached the Union lines after struggling for nine days through a swamp. He asked the people what sustained them during their terrible ordeal. One said, "I saw the lamp of life ahead and the lamp of death behind."[4]

Harriet Tubman left her home in New York to offer her services. She traveled to Beaufort, South Carolina, which had one of the largest concentrations of contraband. She went to Hilton Head, South Carolina, too, where there was also a swelling contraband population. Tubman was promptly assigned to a contraband hospital where many people were suffering from dysentery—severe diarrhea—which could result in dehydration and death. Tubman worked under the command of General David Hunter at

Hilton Head, the headquarters of the Union Army in the South.

Beaufort was a large town, and it was filled with Union soldiers, government agents, and homeless slaves. Tubman's work with the slaves was made more difficult by the fact that they could not understand her well, and she could not understand them. They spoke the Gullah dialect common among blacks in South Carolina. But Tubman patiently made herself understood, and though she had no medical training, she did have a good working knowledge of medicinal herbs. She went to the nearby river and found water lilies, pulling them up root and all. Then she collected crane's bill (geranium). She beat the plants into a powder and boiled the powder into a dark, bitter tea that helped the people suffering from dysentery. The only other medicine available to her at the makeshift hospitals was whisky, which was used as a sedative.

Tubman was given $200 by the army to use for the construction of a washhouse. Once the building was completed, she trained some of the contraband women to do washing for the soldiers, who paid them. This gave many families a source of income. For the first time in their lives they were receiving wages. Only slaves like Harriet Tubman and others with skills such as carpentry or blacksmithing had been rented out by their masters and given the chance to earn wages. Tubman became skilled at logging, but most of the slave women knew only housework.

Tubman herself received no pay from the army. She got room and board and earned a little cash by making and selling root beer, gingerbread, and pies. She made them at night and paid someone to peddle them during the day while she worked at the hospital.

Eventually, Tubman was called to work at a military hospital in Fernandina, Florida, where both soldiers and contraband were, she said, "dying off like sheep," from dysentery.[5] Tubman made more herbal tea and attended to the basic care of the sick, keeping them clean and fed. Far more serious was the smallpox that soon came to ravage the population. Tubman worked relentlessly with the smallpox victims, never herself getting sick. She had no fear of illness or death. She often said, "The Lord will take care of me until my time comes."[6] She would then add that she was always ready to go.

Tubman's days at the hospital were very busy. Her tasks included filling buckets with water and chunks of ice to bathe the heads of the sick and the wounds of the soldiers and civilians. She would bathe three or four people and then the water would become too warm or too bloody to be of any more use. She would then repeat the routine, getting another pail of clean water with ice.

As northern forces moved into the South, they were eager for information about the Confederate strategy and troop movements. Much of this was available from blacks who overheard important information or observed troop movements. But the slaves were often unwilling to talk to northerners. They did not trust them. They often feared the strange white men with their curious accents as much as they had feared their masters. Sometimes slaves fled into the woods at the very sight of the Union soldiers.

Harriet Tubman, however, was able to win the confidence of the slaves and extract information from them. So began her career as a Civil War scout and spy. She accompanied Union expeditions up and down the rivers and into the wilderness, talking to slaves along the way and getting crucial bits and pieces of information. She often went behind Confederate lines, posing as a peddler selling chickens and gingerbread. This gave her extra spending money as well as a logical reason for being there so the Confederate soldiers would not be suspicious.[7]

On one occasion, General Hunter asked Tubman to go on a gunboat up the Combahee River in South Carolina. The purpose of the expedition was to recover torpedoes the Confederate Army had placed there to blow up Yankee gunboats. Tubman had learned the location of the torpedoes from slaves who lived along the river and had observed men placing them. She also knew the location of important Confederate supply depots from her information-gathering forays.

Another purpose of the Combahee River expedition was to destroy southern bridges and railroads, cutting off the supply lines to the Confederate Army.

Harriet Tubman's uniform for these missions was a coat and dress in federal blue, and a large bandanna worn over her short hair. She carried a satchel filled with first-aid equipment, her musket, and canteen. Colonel James Montgomery, an old friend of Tubman's who shared her abolitionist views, led the Combahee River expedition. Later, Montgomery would write his commanding officer praising Tubman as "a most remarkable woman, and invaluable as a scout."[8] As part of the expedition, one hundred fifty black Union soldiers traveled in three steam-powered gunboats.

President Abraham Lincoln issued the Emancipation Proclamation in September 1862 to take effect on January 1, 1863. The proclamation decreed freedom for the slaves in states fighting the United States armies. Beginning in 1863, President Lincoln sought to recruit black soldiers for the Civil War. Many, like the men in the gunboats heading up the Combahee River, flocked to the Union colors.

The expedition was successful in destroying millions of dollars' worth of Confederate supplies, removing dangerous torpedoes, and freeing eight hundred slaves.

Historian Lerone Bennett said that Tubman was "the most remarkable of all Union spies," and the first woman to "lead U.S. Army troops in battle."[9] Bennett may have been referring to the Combahee River expedition as a battle. Though Colonel James Montgomery was the commander, he allowed Tubman to shout out instructions about the Confederate sentry post half a mile up or where to ambush the Confederate rebels who tried to resist.[10]

Colonel Montgomery had organized runaway slaves into army units that would strike inside rebel-held country. From Port Royal, South Carolina, the army sailed up the Combahee River, burning plantations and liberating slaves. Tubman sang a hymn with a chorus beginning "Come along," to reassure and encourage slaves to join them. Although they were under Confederate fire, Montgomery and Tubman and their troops returned without a scratch.

Wendell Phillips, a famous abolitionist, added his praise on Tubman's wartime work. Familiar with her activities in the Civil War, he said that there were few who did more for the cause than "our fearless and most sagacious friend, Harriet Tubman."[11]

Tubman met many black soldiers during the war. One was a tall, handsome recruit named Nelson Davis of Company G of the English U.S. Colored Infantry Volunteers. Tubman told Davis all about herself and her little house in Auburn, New York. Years later, the two would meet again.

The black people who came to Union lines disliked being called "contraband" and were intensely proud to be accepted into the Union Army.[12] One wounded black soldier was walking toward a base hospital loaded down with a shoulder bag, musket, and cartridge box. When someone offered to relieve him of his burden, he refused and insisted on carrying his equipment all the way to the hospital so they would recognize him as a soldier.[13]

Harriet Tubman organized a scouting service for the Union Army under the direct supervision of Secretary of War Edwin Stanton. She picked seven former slaves who knew the inland areas and could locate food-storage sites and Confederate ammunition dumps. Tubman also chose two black river pilots who knew every foot of the terrain. They surveyed the countryside in preparation for raids by black regiments who went up the St. Mary's River, which divided Florida from Georgia. The raids brought back supplies including iron, lumber, bricks, rice, and herds of sheep.

In 1863, the Fifty-fourth Massachusetts Volunteers stormed Fort Wagner in Charleston Harbor. These were the first black troops organized into a combat unit in the Union Army. Harriet Tubman witnessed this battle and later helped carry the wounded and the dead off the battlefield.

A thousand black troops advanced on a narrow causeway. Fort Wagner was a key position in the Confederate defense of Charleston, South Carolina. The first assault was made on July 11, 1863, and the heaviest fighting took place on July 18. All the soldiers of the Fifty-fourth—1,354 men—participated. In spite of their brave efforts, the initial attack failed and there were 247 casualties. The bombardment of Fort Wagner continued until it fell to Union forces in August 1863.[14] The bravery of these soldiers convinced northerners that they should accept black soldiers.[15]

Harriet Tubman described the battle in graphic detail. The guns, she said, were like lightning, and the big guns like thunder. Tubman compared going onto the battlefield when the guns were silent to getting in the crops. "It was dead men that we reaped," she said.[16] "And then we heard the rain falling and that was the drops of blood," Tubman recalled.[17]

Sergeant William Carney, flag bearer for the Fifty-fourth Volunteers, took bullets to his head, chest, arm, and leg. He said proudly, as he lay wounded, "The old flag never touched the ground, boys."[18] Carney's poignant boast about upholding the honor of the flag became a rallying cry for other soldiers.

He won the Congressional Medal of Honor, along with twenty-two other black soldiers, but it took him thirty-seven years to receive it. Prejudice against black soldiers persisted for many years and they were long denied the honors due them.

Tubman's Civil War activities—working as a spy, scout, soldier, and nurse—never drained her sturdy constitution. In her mid-forties during the war, she was about twice the age of most of the young men she tended after the battle. She walked among people with highly contagious diseases and was close to the battlefield, but she seemed to lead "a charmed life."[19]

Early in 1864, another black crusader for freedom, the legendary Sojourner Truth, met Tubman in Boston. Truth was on her way to Washington to see President Lincoln, and Tubman was taking time out to visit her parents in New York. Truth's biographer, Nell Painter, believed the two women had much in common. Both shared a devotion to their people, said Painter, and "adventurous pasts, intimate connection with God, singing and ways of knowing independent of literacy."[20] However, Tubman and Truth disagreed on the character of President Lincoln. Truth saw Lincoln as a friend of black people, but Tubman resented the fact that emancipation had been delayed, and she believed that white soldiers received more money than blacks during the Civil War.[21]

Chapter 9

A NEW BEGINNING

In the spring of 1865, Harriet Tubman began working as a nurse at a veterans hospital in Fort Monroe, Virginia. She was employed by the United States Sanitary Commission, a civilian organization that made private homes and hospitals available for wounded soldiers. The Army Medical Bureau lacked the funds to care for these veterans.

Tubman soon found that the hospital lacked necessary medical supplies. The only sedative available was whisky. When a man's leg had to be amputated, it was Tubman's job to hold him down while the surgeon worked. A lead bullet was placed in the man's mouth for him to bite down on. It was often bitten in half during the agonizing ordeal. In July

1865, Tubman left the hospital and went to Washington to protest conditions at Fort Monroe and other veterans hospitals which were woefully short of funds.

Her job at Fort Monroe was Tubman's last official work for the government or private agencies serving the Civil War veterans. Through it all, as nurse, spy, and scout, she had received no pay for her services. She had cooked and nursed and guided the gunboats down the Combahee River, but the government never paid her. Tubman figured it all out and came to the conclusion that she was due about $1,800 from the United States government for her services.[1]

When Tubman prepared to leave Washington to return home, she was given a government half-fare pass to ride the train. But when she took her seat in the passenger car, the conductor came through and challenged her right to sit there. He could not accept that a plain-looking, poorly dressed black woman had actually received a government pass to ride at half fare. He ordered Tubman to go and sit in the baggage car. Tubman refused to move and the conductor enlisted the help of three other men to grab her and drag her to the baggage car, where she rode the rest of the way to Auburn. During the struggle the men wrenched Tubman's arm and shoulder so violently that she suffered pain for a long time afterward.

Tubman, about forty-four years old, was returning to Auburn. She had no clear means of support, and no activity would consume her life as the Underground Railroad had.

Tubman arrived home with no money, but she still had her parents to support. She was determined to make their lives as comfortable as possible. She planted a vegetable garden and apple trees in the yard, hoping to sell the produce and earn income that way. A few donations from white friends saw Tubman and her parents through her first few months home. For herself, Tubman wanted no luxuries. She dressed in the simplest clothes and ate plain food, expressing a desire for a piece of fruit now and then.[2]

With the Civil War over, and slavery conquered, Tubman embraced another cause: woman suffrage—the right to vote. She believed that the issue of blacks' rights to equality was linked to woman suffrage.[3] Tubman said, "I have suffered enough" to believe in women's right to vote.[4] Many of Tubman's ardent abolitionist supporters were also suffragists, so this cause was always close to her heart.

In October 1867, along a road in Dorchester County, Maryland, John Tubman, Harriet Tubman's former husband, had a fight with a white man named Robert Vincent. There is no record of what the fight was about, but Vincent told Tubman that if he ever saw him again, he would kill him. Apparently, Tubman made no effort to stay away from Vincent despite the threat, and they met again. Vincent drew his gun and deliberately shot John Tubman. Vincent was indicted and tried for murder, but he was acquitted. The only witness to the incident was Tubman's thirteen-year-old son, and the testimony of black people held little weight in Maryland at that time. Harriet Tubman heard of her husband's death. She had long since lost any affection for him, but she had been his wife and now she was a widow.

In the winter of 1867–1868, a severe blizzard buried many of the houses in Auburn, including Tubman's. Tubman and her parents, being poor, had few extra provisions, and the pantry was quickly emptied while they were snowed in. Tubman had never asked for help for herself, but this time she had to. Eventually, she struggled from the snowbound house and made her way to town. She asked a friend for a quarter with which to buy food. With that, Tubman was able to buy a little food for herself and her parents. A few days later, Tubman returned the quarter, paying her friend back in full. Tubman had been able to earn a little money by helping neighbors dig out from the snow.

Though she was living in deep poverty herself, with no money set aside and no income, Tubman dreamed of being able to help others, especially the poor, homeless, and sick among the black population. Many were former slaves who had toiled most of their lives expecting support in their old age. As bad as slavery was, it had provided for elderly slaves with no other means of support. Of course, it had also deprived them of the education and opportunity to build their own security. This generation of emancipated slaves was now caught in the middle—uneducated, illiterate, floundering, and destitute. These were the people Tubman wanted to help.

Tubman never refused to help anyone who came to her door, and come they did. Her generosity was well known and her little house was usually filled with half a dozen or more strangers needing assistance. Occasionally, Tubman's old friends would send her money. But Tubman had a carefree attitude about money, according to fellow Auburnites familiar with her charitable ways. She would receive a windfall and then give it all away, trusting in the Lord to replace it when needed.[5]

To support herself and her parents, Tubman nursed sick neighbors, did a little bit of housecleaning, and cared for neighborhood children when she was needed. As her garden grew, she sold vegetables door-to-door in season and also sold chickens and eggs.

By then, Tubman's parents were about eighty, and they could not be of much help. Once, when a friend came to visit, Tubman was taking care of her parents, a brother, a grandniece, several elderly black people, and several children. At times the house would bulge with as many as twenty people, all looking to Tubman for support.

A temporary rescue came to Tubman from a white Auburn schoolteacher, the daughter of a professor at Auburn Theological Seminary. In 1868, Sarah Hopkins Bradford, who was sympathetic to Tubman's works, devised a plan to channel some money to her. During the years that Tubman was away helping the Union win the Civil War, Bradford had tended to Tubman's parents, making sure they were provided for and writing letters for them. (Most of their letters were to their daughter Harriet, asking her when she was coming home.) Now, with Tubman home and in desperate need of funds, Bradford decided that a book about this remarkable woman might be a way of raising money for her.

Bradford sat down in Tubman's little house and listened to stories of her childhood, the experiences she had in the

Underground Railroad, and her exploits during the Civil War. Bradford wrote the stories down, but, although she trusted Tubman's honesty, some of the stories were almost too amazing to be true. So with a scholar's rigorous integrity, the teacher checked and double-checked every story Tubman told her, interviewing other people who had played a part in the events. "I have received corroboration of every incident related to me by my heroic friend," Bradford wrote.[6] She even omitted some incidents—wonderful, exciting stories that she believed to be true—that could not be verified. Bradford wrote her first book in 1868, titled *Scenes in the Life of Harriet Tubman*. Later she wrote a more complete book, *Harriet Tubman: The Moses of Her People*. Bradford wrote quickly because Tubman needed financial help right away The first edition of the little book was printed in 1869 with funds from Tubman's friends Garrett Smith and Wendell Phillips and from some businessmen in Auburn. Sales of the book brought about $1,200 and Bradford gave all the money to Tubman. She was able to pay off her mortgage, help some struggling black schools, and feed more hungry wayfarers at her door. For a while the burden of extreme poverty was lifted from her shoulders.

In 1869, a young man appeared at Tubman's door, someone she remembered from the Civil War. The handsome young soldier she had met in South Carolina, Nelson Davis, had never forgotten Harriet Tubman. He had kept her Auburn address and now had come for a visit. They immediately struck up a warm friendship talking about old times. Tubman, then forty-nine, and Davis, twenty-eight, grew fond of each other and they courted. On March 18, 1869, Tubman and Davis were married.

It seemed that Tubman had now gained a strong, healthy helpmate who would ease her struggles. Unfortunately, that was not to be. Soon after their marriage, Davis fell ill with tuberculosis, a serious disease that affects the lungs. His illness lingered throughout the rest of his life. He was not able to work at all during their nineteen-year marriage, and Tubman was his caretaker until the day he finally died of tuberculosis. She bore this difficult obligation with the same quiet, uncomplaining courage she had exhibited in everything else she did. When Nelson Davis died in 1888, Tubman was a widow again.

In 1870, Harriet Tubman's parents, though in their nineties, still walked about a mile every Sunday to attend services at the Central Church. Then they went to a class meeting at the Methodist Church, and finally a third service at another church before heading home. Harriet Tubman usually sang at these services.

The Rosses died in 1871, both nearly one hundred years old. Tubman's faithful friend William Seward, a former governor of New York, died in 1872. He had helped her bring her parents to Canada and to buy the house in Auburn, New York. Seward added greatly to Tubman's peace of mind at times when she needed help the most. Once he told her that she had worked for others long enough and now he wanted her to ask him for something that would benefit her alone. But Tubman could not think of anything she wanted just for herself.[7] When Seward died, Tubman was deeply moved and wanted to show her respect. She traveled alone to Washington for his funeral. It was a great occasion, with Seward's flower-bedecked casket surrounded by many famous people as well as family and friends. Quietly, almost unnoticed, the small, sturdy figure of a black woman moved to the casket, paused, and placed a wreath of field flowers at the great man's feet. It was all Harriet Tubman had to give to her dead friend and ally. Then she slipped away, her debt of gratitude for his compassion toward her people paid.

Tubman's dream of building a home for poor, helpless blacks continued, but she lacked the funds. Her main source of income continued to be peddling the produce from her garden.

In 1898, Tubman was about seventy-eight years old. (In a letter written for her, she said she was about seventy-five, but she did not know for sure.) Once again, driven by the desire to help people, she pleaded with the government to pay her what she was owed for the years she had served during the Civil War. She had worked for the government in many capacities, from nurse to scout, and she expected to be compensated.

Harriet Tubman's struggle to get her rightful compensation from the government continued for a long time. Back in 1868, Charles P. Wood, a prominent New Yorker who sympathized with Tubman's situation, had first mounted a campaign to get the money due her. He compiled a large dossier of letters from Civil War officers Tubman had served under, affirming her valuable service.[8]

V. K. Barnes, the surgeon general, affirmed that Tubman had been a nurse and matron at the colored hospital in Macon, Georgia, that served contraband. Brigadier General Rufus Saxton wrote a letter verifying her service as nurse and spy, saying that she had been on many raids behind enemy lines, adding that she displayed "remarkable courage, zeal and fidelity."[9]

Included in the dossier were passes that Tubman had received, giving her permission to go behind military lines during the war. One authorized her to receive bourbon whisky for medicinal purposes. Others approved free passage for her on military transports as she carried out her duties. There was no doubt, based on the mass of evidence, that Tubman had been in the employ of the United States government, during important work.

William Seward had placed a letter in the 1869 packet as well, saying that Tubman had been "nursing our soldiers during nearly all the war."[10]

In spite of all this evidence and years of appeal, Tubman received no compensation for her own service during the Civil War.[11] The only pension that Tubman did receive was $8 a month as the widow of a Civil War soldier. Nelson Davis had served from September 1863 to November 1865 and as his widow, Tubman was entitled to a pension. After the most prominent citizens of Auburn signed a petition and sent it to the representative from Tubman's district, an Act of Congress increased her widow's pension from $8 to $20 a month.[12]

In 1897, a Senate Committee recommended that she also be given $25 a month for her *own* service to the government. But this did not happen.

In the late 1890s, Tubman was a delegate to the first convention of the National Federation of Afro American women (later called the National Association of Colored Women). She also had a reception in her honor at the New England Women Suffrage Association.[13] Between her husband's pension, and the proceeds of occasional parties given by her friends to raise money for her, Tubman managed to eke out an existence as well as extend help to poor neighbors and destitute strangers. Even into her early eighties, Tubman continued to work with vigor for the causes she believed in and the welfare of the needy.

Chapter 10

I CAN HEAR THE
ANGELS SINGING

Queen Victoria of England, having heard of Harriet Tubman's exploits, sent her a silk shawl and a silver medal in 1897. Queen Victoria invited Tubman to come to London and be honored at a reception, but Tubman never considered going. She could not afford or even fathom taking a trip so far from home. But she did prize the honor that had come from a distant land.

Tubman's dream of a poor people's shelter in Auburn came closer to reality when she was able to buy twenty-five acres adjoining her home. But, though she now owned a large enough property for her dream, she never raised the necessary funds to proceed.

In 1903, Tubman finally faced the fact that she could not build a home for elderly and homeless black people. She then deeded her property to the A.M.E. Zion Church, where she had worshiped for so many years. In 1908, the church built the Harriet Tubman Home for Aged and Indigent Colored People on the twenty-five acres.

Harriet Tubman's face had grown furrowed, and her rheumatism was making it increasingly difficult for her to get around. Her mind and memory remained as sharp as ever, though, and she enjoyed taking care of her own house. Until she reached the age of ninety, she lived in her home and received visitors as usual, regaling all who came with vivid stories of her experiences. There was always a steady stream of visitors.

In 1911, the Empire State Federation of Women held a linen shower for Tubman, collecting many good items, which Tubman shared with others.[1] This women's club also voted to send Tubman $25 a month for the rest of her life. But Tubman's life was running out.

On May 19, 1911, Tubman was no longer able to live alone and take care of herself, so she moved into the home she had helped found for others. For about three months she had been an invalid in her own house, struggling to survive without help, in spite of her growing infirmities. She realized it was time to face facts and get help. Edward Brooks, general superintendent of the home and an A.M.E. Zion clergyman, said, "It is the desire of the Home management to give her every attention and comfort possible in these last days."[2]

Tubman's friends came to visit her at the home, and one day she told some members of the A.M.E. Zion Church that she felt her death was near. Her deep religious faith, which had never wavered at any time in her long life, made the nearness of death joyful rather than fearful. "I can hear the bells a'ringing," she told her visitors. "I can hear the angels singing. I can see the hosts a'marching."[3]

In March 1913, Tubman fell ill with pneumonia. Her friends gathered at her bedside to sing hymns and offer comfort. On March 10, 1913, Harriet Tubman died. She was about ninety-three years old.

The Empire State Federation of Women, which had taken such great interest in Tubman, paid for her funeral and later for a headstone to be placed at her grave.[4] Most of the people of Auburn attended Tubman's funeral, and a military band played taps as she was laid to rest. At last, there was recognition of the important role she had played in the Union's victory over the Confederacy and the resulting emancipation of Tubman's people. She was honored as all fallen comrades were honored.

On June 14, 1914, one year after Harriet Tubman's death, the Auburn local post of the Grand Army of the Republic led the city in a memorial celebration of her life. Most of the townspeople flew American flags in her honor while the mayor, Charles W. Brister, recalled her as "one who suffered for the cause of freedom."[5] The main speaker was the famed African-American leader and educator Booker T. Washington, who paid tribute to Tubman as one who "brought the two races together."[6]

In 1982, Charles L. Blockson, the African-American author and illustrator of several books on black history, described his own emotional visit to Tubman's grave in Auburn, New York. Of the grove of trees where she is buried, Blockson wrote, "The trees seem to comfort her and shield her from unwanted notice." Blockson was moved to tears as he touched the gravestone and recalled Tubman's "nineteen mosquito plagued and frostbitten journeys leading others to freedom."[7]

Tubman's obituary in the *Afro American Ledger* on March 15, 1913, referred to her as the "Queen of the Underground" and said that in many ways she had proved herself to be one of the "foremost women in her times."[8]

Tributes to Tubman came from black and white alike. Abolitionist Thomas Wentworth Higginson called Harriet Tubman "the greatest heroine of the age."[9] William Still, the famous black leader of the Underground Railroad who had worked so often with Tubman, lauded her "adventurous spirit" that was "wholly without fear."[10] Twentieth-century black author Benjamin Quarles wrote that of all the blacks who worked the Underground Railroad, all names "pale before that of Harriet Tubman."[11]

Author Samuel Hopkins said of Tubman that "no fear of the lash, the bloodhound, or the fiery stake" could stop her from helping her people to freedom.[12]

Harriet Tubman was largely unsung during her incredible life. She was revered by a small group of white abolitionists and known by many poor slaves who loved her and were inspired by her but had no means to publicize her life.

William Seward said of Tubman, "A nobler, higher spirit, or a truer, seldom dwells in human form."[13]

Perhaps the most powerful tribute of all came from another former slave who, like Tubman, had fled from the whip and the chains. Frederick Douglass took notice of the fact that Tubman, unlike himself and other eloquent fighters against slavery, labored mostly in secrecy. She never received the widespread public praise that was given to Douglass. Douglass said that her deeds of courage and compassion were seen firsthand only by a "few trembling, scarred, footsore bondmen and women," and he pointed out that "the midnight sky and silent stars have been the witnesses of your devotion to freedom and of your heroism."[14]

After Tubman's death, African Americans in Boston founded the Harriet Tubman Home to serve the needs of destitute black women. Schoolteacher Pauline E. Hopkins wrote in *Colored American Magazine* that few people on earth were so motivated by the cause that possessed Tubman throughout her life "to lay our time, talents and opportunities for God's glory and the good of our fellow men."[15]

In the years since Harriet Tubman's death, honors and recognition have come in many forms. Famed black baritone Paul Robeson, when singing the spiritual "Go Down Moses," always talked of Tubman's special use of this hymn. Folksinger Woodie Guthrie composed "The Ballad of Harriet Tubman," and composers Robert De Cormier and Donald McKay wrote a cantata based on her life, which they titled "They Called Her Moses."

Tubman has been an important subject for many African American artists. Aaron Douglass made Tubman the subject of a mural, and Charles White painted a portrait of her in Chinese ink and wash titled *General Moses*. Jacob Lawrence created thirty tempera paintings on a Tubman theme. Artist Hughie Lee Smith tried to learn as much as possible about Tubman before painting her. As a result of this research, he said he came "to love this woman."[16]

During World War II, President Franklin D. Roosevelt praised the U.S. Maritime Commission for choosing the name *Harriet Tubman* for a liberty ship. This was especially appropriate given the expedition Tubman took up the Combahee River on a gunboat during the Civil War. In 1974, the Department of the Interior gave Tubman's home in Auburn the status of National Historic Landmark.

In 1978, a first-class Harriet Tubman postage stamp was introduced, the first in the Black Heritage USA series.

Anyone studying the life of the courageous and unassuming Harriet Tubman would have to agree with a young teacher, Charlotte L. Forten, who met Tubman at Beaufort, South Carolina, during the Civil War. "She is a wonderful woman—a real heroine," Forten said.[17]

After decades of neglecting her legacy, more and more people are recognizing Harriet Tubman's contribution. In Dick Russell's book *Black Genius and the American Experience*, he quotes legendary jazz musician Wynton Marsalis. The trumpeter was asked which human being best exemplified heroism in American history. Marsalis was born in 1961 and represents a newer generation that is coming to appreciate Tubman. He said, "She's a real democratic figure. She kept goin' back. If she'd ever got caught, mannnnn! She was a woman, which was even harder. I think Robeson and Du Bois got tired. Harriet Tubman didn't get tired."[18]

CHRONOLOGY

1820?—Harriet Tubman is born in Dorchester County, Maryland.

1835—Sustains a severe head injury when struck by a lead weight.

1844—Marries John Tubman.

1849—Escapes slavery and moves to Pennsylvania.

1850—Begins work with the Underground Railroad; Fugitive Slave Law is passed.

1851—Rescues sister and her family from Maryland; helps her brother John Ross escape.

1854—Helps three of her brothers escape to Canada.

1857—Rescues parents and brings them to Canada; acquires house in Auburn, New York.

1858—Meets with John Brown.

1861—Civil War begins and Tubman begins her work as a nurse, spy, and scout.

1863—Witnesses Fort Wagner battle (Charleston, South Carolina) and serves as nurse for the wounded; Emancipation Proclamation is issued.

1864—Meets with Sojourner Truth.

1865—Works for U.S. Sanitary Commission at Fort Monroe, Virginia.

1869—Publication of biography *Harriet Tubman: The Moses of Her People*, by Sarah Bradford; Tubman marries Nelson Davis.

1888—Death of Nelson Davis.

1896—Serves as delegate to first convention of National Federation of Afro American Women.

1908—Harriet Tubman Home for Aged and Indigent Colored People opens.

1913—Dies on March 10, 1913.

CHAPTER NOTES

Chapter 1. The Next Time Moses Comes

1. Sarah Bradford, *Harriet Tubman: The Moses of Her People* (Gloucester, Mass.: Peter Smith, 1981; first published in 1869), p. 40.

2. Ibid., p. 41.

3. Ibid.

4. Charles L. Blockson, *The Underground Railroad* (New York: Prentice Hall, 1987), p. 105.

5. Ibid.

6. Ibid., p. 99.

7. Bradford, p. 48.

8. *Afro American Encyclopedia* (Miami, Florida: Educational Book Publishing, 1974), vol. 9, p. 2652.

9. Bradford, p. 53.

10. Samuel Eliot Morison, *The Oxford History of the American People* (New York: Oxford University Press, 1965), p. 521.

Chapter 2. Like a Weed

1. *African American Biography* (Detroit: Gale Research, Inc., 1993), vol. 4, p. 731.

2. Dick Russell, *Black Genius and the American Experience* (New York: Carroll and Graf Publishers, Inc., 1998), p. 409.

3. Sarah Bradford, *Harriet Tubman: The Moses of Her People* (Gloucester, Mass.: Peter Smith, 1981; first published in 1869), p. 69.

4. Benjamin Quarles, "Harriet Tubman," in Leon Litwick and August Meier, eds., *Black Leaders of the Nineteenth Century* (Chicago: University of Illinois Press, 1982), p. 44.

5. *African American Biography*, p. 731.

6. Quarles, p. 52.

7. Charles L. Blockson, *The Underground Railroad* (New York: Prentice Hall, 1987), p. 118.

8. Ibid.

9. Ibid.

10. Ibid.

11. Lerone Bennett, *Wade in the Water: Great Moments in Black History* (Chicago: Johnson Publishing Company, 1979), p. 86.

12. *African American Biography*, p. 731.

13. Bradford, p. 23.

14. Bennett, p. 86.

Chapter 3. Liberty or Death

1. John Hope Franklin, *From Slavery to Freedom* (New York: Alfred Knopf, 1974), p. 184.

2. Sarah Bradford, *Harriet Tubman: The Moses of Her People* (Gloucester, Mass.: Peter Smith, 1981; first published in 1869), p. 129.

3. Ibid., p. 24.

4. Ibid.

5. Ibid., pp. 25-26.

6. *Afro American Encyclopedia* (Miami, Florida: Educational Book Publishing, Inc., 1974), vol. 9, p. 2651.

7. Charles L. Blockson, *The Underground Railroad* (New York: Prentice Hall, 1987), p. 119.

8. Ibid.

9. Ibid.

10. Ibid.

11. Bradford, p. 29.

12. *African American Biography* (Detroit, Michigan: Gale Research, Inc., 1993), vol. 4., p. 732.

13. *Afro American Encyclopedia*, p. 2651.

Chapter 4. The Conductor

1. Sarah Bradford, *Harriet Tubman: The Moses of Her People* (Gloucester, Mass.: Peter Smith, 1981; first published in 1869), p. 31.

2. *Afro American Encyclopedia* (Miami, Florida: Educational Book Publishing, 1974), vol. 9, p. 2651.

3. Lerone Bennett, *Wade in the Water: Great Moments in Black History* (Chicago: Johnson Publishing Company, Inc., 1979), p. 85

4. *Afro American Encyclopedia*, p. 2651.

5. Benjamin Quarles, "Harriet Tubman," in Leon Litwick and August Meier, eds., *Black Leaders of the Nineteenth Century* (Chicago: University of Illinois Press, 1981), pp. 44-45.

6. Charles L. Blockson, *The Underground Railroad* (New York: Prentice Hall, 1987), p. 119.

7. Ibid.

8. Ibid.

9. Ibid.

Chapter 5. Let My People Go

1. Charles L. Blockson, *The Underground Railroad* (New York: Prentice Hall, 1987), p. 98.

2. William Still, *The Underground Railroad* (Chicago: Johnson Publishing Company, Inc., 1970), pp. 305-307.

3. William Breyfogle, *Make Free* (New York: J. B. Lippincott Company, Inc., 1958), p. 192.

4. Mortimer Adler, *The Negro in American History* (New York: Encyclopedia Britannica, 1969), vol. 1, p. 121.

5. Ibid.

6. Dick Russell, *Black Genius and the American Experience* (New York: Carroll and Graf Publishers, Inc., 1998), p. 409.

7. Lerone Bennett, *Wade in the Water: Great Moments in Black History* (Chicago: Johnson Publishing Company, Inc., 1979), p. 82.

8. Blockson, p. 121.

9. Benjamin Quarles, "Harriet Tubman," in Leon Litwick and August Meier, eds., *Black Leaders of the Nineteenth Century* (Chicago: University of Illinois Press, 1982), p. 48.

10. Breyfogle, p. 175.

11. W. E. B. Du Bois, *Du Bois* (New York: The Library of America, 1986), p. 961.

12. Blockson, p. 172.

13. Ibid., p. 173.

14. Ibid., p. 174.

15. Ibid., p. 172-173.

16. Sarah Bradford, *Harriet Tubman: The Moses of Her People* (Gloucester, Mass.: Peter Smith, 1981; first published in 1869), p. 53.

17. Ibid., p. 54.

Chapter 6. You Will Be Free or Die

1. Sarah Bradford, *Harriet Tubman: The Moses of Her People* (Gloucester, Mass.: Peter Smith, 1981; first published in 1869), p. 55.

2. Ibid., p. 57.

3. Ibid., p. 114.

4. Ibid., p. 115.

5. Dick Russell, *Black Genius and the American Experience* (New York: Carroll and Graf Publishers, Inc., 1998), p. 409.

6. *Afro American Encyclopedia* (Miami, Florida: Educational Book Publishing, Inc., 1974), vol. 9, p. 2652.

7. *African American Biography* (Detroit, Mich.: Gale Research, Inc., 1993), vol. 4, p. 732.

8. Charles L. Blockson, *The Underground Railroad* (New York: Prentice Hall, 1987), p. 121.

9. Ibid.

10. Ibid., p. 99.

11. Lereone Bennett, *Wade in the Water: Great Moments in Black History* (Chicago: Johnson Publishing Company, Inc., 1979), p. 84.

12. William Breyfogle, *Make Free* (New York: J. B. Lippincott Company, Inc., 1958), p. 210.

13. Ibid., p. 212.

Chapter 7. The Last Days of the Railroad

1. "A Champion of Freedom," brochure published by the Harriet Tubman Home Tour, p. 1.

2. Charles L. Blockson, *The Underground Railroad* (New York: Prentice Hall, 1987), p. 174.

3. William Still, *The Underground Railroad* (Chicago: Johnson Publishing Company, Inc., 1970), p. 411.

4. W. E. B. Du Bois, *Du Bois* (New York: The Library of America, 1986), p. 960.

5. Benjamin Quarles, "Harriet Tubman," in Leon Litwick and August Meier, eds., *Black Leaders of the Nineteenth Century* (Chicago: University of Illinois Press, 1982), p. 53.

6. Ibid., p. 48.

7. Lynn Sherr and Jurate Kazickas, *Susan B. Anthony Slept Here* (New York: Random House, 1994), p. 301.

8. Sarah Bradford, *Harriet Tubman: The Moses of Her People* (Gloucester, Mass.: Peter Smith, 1981; first published in 1869), p. 136.

9. Ibid., p. 118.

10. Ibid., pp. 133-134.

11. *Afro American Encyclopedia* (Miami, Florida: Educational Book Publisher, 1974), vol. 9, p. 2653.

12. Bradford, p. 122.

13. Ibid.

14. Du Bois, p. 961.

15. Bradford, p. 136.

Chapter 8. Scout, Spy, Nurse, Soldier

1. Sarah Bradford, *Harriet Tubman: The Moses of Her People* (Gloucester. Mass.: Peter Smith, 1981; first published in 1869), p. 92.

2. Ibid., p. 93.

3. Benjamin Quarles, "Harriet Tubman," in Leon Litwick and August Meier, eds., *Black Leaders of the Nineteenth Century* (Chicago: University of Illinois Press, 1982), p. 55.

4. Bruce Catton, *The Army of the Potomac: A Stillness at Appomattox* (Garden City, N.Y.: Doubleday, 1953), p. 230.

5. Bradford, p. 98.

6. Ibid.

7. Jack Salzman et al., *Encyclopedia of African American Culture* (New York: Simon & Schuster, 1996), p. 2677.

8. Bradford, p. 138.

9. Columbus Salley, *The Black 100* (New York: Citadel Press, 1993), p. 51.

10. Philip Sterling and Rayford Logan, *Four Took Freedom* (New York: Doubleday, 1967), pp. 27-28.

11. Bradford, p. 134.

12. Catton, p. 231.

13. Ibid.

14. Richard C. Wade, *Negroes in American Life* (Boston: Houghton Mifflin Company, Inc., 1970), p. 80.

15. "Civil War," *The World Book Multimedia Encyclopedia* (Chicago: World Book, Inc., 1996).

16. Dick Russell, *Black Genius and the American Experience* (New York: Carroll and Graf Publishers, Inc., 1998), p. 108.

17. Ibid.

18. Rayford Logan and Irving Cohen, *The American Negro* (Boston: Houghton Mifflin Company, Inc., 1970), p. 107.

19. Benjamin Quarles, *The Negro in the Making of America* (New York: Macmillan Publishing Company, Inc., 1987), p. 80.

20. Russell, p. 415.

21. Ibid.

Chapter 9. A New Beginning

1. Philip Sterling and Ray Ford Logan, *Four Took Freedom* (New York: Doubleday, 1967), p. 28.

2. Charles L. Blockson, *The Underground Railroad* (New York: Prentice Hall, 1987), p. 123.

3. Jack Salzman, et al., *Encyclopedia of African American Culture* (New York: Simon & Schuster, 1996), p. 2677.

4. Benjamin Quarles, "Harriet Tubman," in Leon Litwick and August Meier, eds., *Black Leaders of the Nineteenth Century* (Chicago: University of Illinois Press, 1982), p. 55.

5. Ibid., p. 95.

6. Sarah Bradford, *Harriet Tubman: The Moses of Her People* (Gloucester, Mass.: Peter Smith, 1981; first published in 1869), p. 5.

7. Ibid., p. 89.

8. Ibid., pp. 139-142.

9. Ibid., 142.

10. Ibid., 137.

11. Herbert Aptheker, *A Documentary History of the Negro People in the United States* (New York: Citadel Press, 1998), vol. 2, p. 781.

12. Megan McClard, *Harriet Tubman: Slavery and the Underground Railroad* (New York: Simon & Schuster, Inc., 1991), p. 123.

13. Jack Salzman et al., *Encyclopedia of African American Culture* (New York: Simon & Schuster, 1996), p. 267.

Chapter 10. I Can Hear the Angels Singing

1. Benjamin Quarles, "Harriet Tubman," in Leon Litwick and August Meier, eds., *Black Leaders of the Nineteenth Century* (Chicago: University of Illinois Press, 1982), p. 50.

2. Ibid., p. 51.

3. Lerone Bennett, *Wade in the Water: Great Moments in Black History* (Chicago: Johnson Publishing Company, Inc., 1979), p. 94.

4. Quarles, p. 51.

5. Ibid., p. 56.

6. Ibid.

7. Charles L. Blockson, *The Underground Railroad* (New York: Prentice Hall, 1987), p. x.

8. Quarles, p. 47.

9. Bennett, p. 87.

10. Ibid.

11. Benjamin Quarles, "Forward to the 1970 edition," William Still, *The Underground Railroad* (Chicago: Johnson Publishing Company, Inc., 1970), p. v.

12. Columbus Salley, *The Black 100* (New York: Citadel Press, 1993), p. 49.

13. Sarah Bradford, *Harriet Tubman: The Moses of Her People* (Gloucester, Mass.: Peter Smith, 1981; first published in 1869), p. 76.

14. William S. McFeely, *Frederick Douglass* (New York: W. W. Norton and Company, Inc. 1991), p. 263.

15. Quarles, p. 52.

16. Ibid., p. 57.

17. Ibid., p. 49.

18. Dick Russell, *Black Genius and the American Experience* (New York: Carroll and Graf Publishers, Inc., 1995), p. 63.

FURTHER READING

Bennett, Lerone, Jr. *Wade in the Water: Great Moments in Black History*. Chicago: Johnson Publishing Company, Inc., 1979.

Blockson, Charles L. *The Underground Railroad*. New York: Prentice Hall, 1987.

Bradford, Sarah. *Harriet Tubman: The Moses of Her People*. Gloucester, Mass.: Peter Smith, 1981 (first published in 1869).

Childress, Alice. *When the Rattlesnake Sounds*. New York: Coward McCann, 1975.

McClard, Megan. *Harriet Tubman: Slavery and the Underground Railroad*. New York: Simon & Schuster, Inc., 1991.

McGovern, Ann. *Runaway Slave: The Story of Harriet Tubman*. New York: Four Winds Press, 1965.

Quarles, Benjamin. *The Negro in the Making of America*. New York: Macmillan Publishing Company, Inc., 1987.

Russell, Dick. *Black Genius and the American Experience*. New York: Carroll and Graf Publishers, Inc., 1998.

Schroeder, Alan. *Minty: A Story of a Young Harriet Tubman*. New York: Dial Books, 1996.

Taylor, Marion. *Harriet Tubman: Antislavery Activist*. Philadelphia: Chelsea House Publishers, 1991.

INDEX

Montgomery, James, 62–64

N
Nalle, Charles, 54–56
National Federation of Afro
American Women, 76

P
Philadelphia, Pennsylvania, 8,
25–27, 29–30, 45, 50
Philadelphia Vigilance
Committee, 26–27, 29
Phillips, Wendell, 64, 72

R
rice plantation, 12, 20, 42
Robeson, Paul, 81, 83
Roosevelt, Franklin, 82
Ross, Benjamin (father), 9–10,
14, 18, 47, 48, 50–51, 73
Ross, Harriet "Rit" (mother),
9–10, 18, 50–51, 73
Ross, John (brother), 29

S
Saxton, Rufus, 75
*Scenes in the Life of Harriet
Tubman*, 72
Seward, William, 51, 73–75, 81
slave auctions, 28
slave cabins, 10
slave reward posters, 35
Smith, Garrett, 72
Smith, Hughie, 82
Stanton, Edwin, 64
Stewart, John, 14–15
Still, William, 26–27, 33, 50,
80
Sumner, Charles, 53

T
Thompson, Anthony, 22, 50
Tubman, Harriet
birth, 10
childhood, 9–16
Civil War work, 59–66,
67–68
death, 79
head injury, 14
marriages, 19–20, 72–73
postage stamp, 82
Underground Railroad,
25–57
woman suffrage, 69
Tubman, John (husband),
18–20, 22, 27, 30, 69
Tubman, Richard, 18
Truth, Sojourner, 52, 66
Turner, Nat, 15

U
Underground Railroad, 7,
17–18, 26–28, 31, 36,
38–41, 45, 52, 54, 57, 68,
72, 80
maps, **23**, **49**

V
Victoria, Queen, 77

W
Washington, Booker T., 79
White, Charles, 82
Wood, Charles P., 74